GOD'S BOOK OF FAITH

God's Book of Faith

Meditations from Job

By
Herbert Lockyer

Published in Nashville, Tennessee, by Thomas Nelson, Inc., and
distributed in Canada by Lawson Falle, Ltd.,
Cambridge, Ontario.

Printed in the United States of America

Unless otherwise noted, all scripture quotations are from THE NEW KING
JAMES VERSION. Copyright © 1979, 1980, 1982, Thomas Nelson, Inc.,
Publishers.

Scripture quotations noted kjv are from the King James Version of the
Bible.

Library of Congress Cataloging in Publication Data

Lockyer, Herbert.
God's book of faith.

1. Bible. O.T. Job—Criticism, interpretation,
etc. 2. Bible. O.T. Job—Meditations. I. Title.
BS1415.2.L63 1986 223'.106 86-23537
ISBN 0-8407-5893-0

Thomas Nelson Publishers
Nashville • Camden • New York

Published in Nashville, Tennessee, by Thomas Nelson, Inc. and
distributed in Canada by Lawson Falle, Ltd.,
Cambridge, Ontario.

Printed in the United States of America.

Unless otherwise noted, all Scripture quotations are from THE NEW KING
JAMES VERSION. Copyright © 1979, 1980, 1982, Thomas Nelson, Inc.,
Publishers.

Scripture quotations noted KJV are from the King James Version of the
Bible.

Library of Congress Cataloging in Publication Data

Lockyer, Herbert.
  God's book of faith.

  1. Bible. O.T. Job—Criticism, interpretation,
etc. 2. Bible. O.T. Job—Meditations. I. Title.
BS1415.2.L63 1984   223'.106   84-2161

ISBN: 978-0-8407-5893-4

TO
Leonard and Norah Thurlow

With gratitude to God
For their lives and witness

TO
Leonard and Norah Thurlow

With gratitude to God
For their lives and witness

Contents

Introduction

For centuries the remarkable Book of Job has been classed as a masterpiece in the realms of literature, theology, and morals. Volumes have been written about it that would require the patience of Job to read and digest. The greatest minds of all ages have extolled its unique literary charm and spiritual value. For me, it has risen above all other books, just as Joseph's sheaf rose higher than those of his brethren.

Thomas Carlyle, renowned nineteenth-century Scottish literary critic and historian, in his fascinating work *On Heroes, Hero-Worship, and the Heroic in History* paid this tribute to Job:

> I call this book, apart from all theories about it, one of the grandest books ever written with pen. A noble book—all men's Book! . . . There is nothing written, I think, in the Bible, or out of it, of equal literary merit.

It is said that toward the close of his life, Carlyle sat waiting for tea one evening, with a Bible in his hand. Then he was observed burying himself once more in the pages of that same Book of Job, which he had once called "the oldest choral melody of the heart of mankind."

Tennyson, the master poet, called the Book of Job "The greatest poem, whether of ancient or modern literature."

9

Martin Luther, the renowned reformer, regarded it in this way: "More magnificent and sublime than any other book of Scripture."

John J. Ingalls, for eighteen years a United States senator from Kansas, once remarked, "My favorite part of the Bible is the Book of Job."

Samuel Rutherford, the saintly Scottish preacher, found consolation on his deathbed from Job 13:15, "Though He slay me, yet will I trust Him," and he cried out in ecstasy:

> If He should slay me ten thousand times, ten thousand times I'll trust Him. I feel, I feel, I believe in joy, and rejoice; I feed on manna. O, for arms to embrace Him! O, for a well-tuned harp!

William Jennings Bryan, Democratic nominee for the American presidency in 1896 and also in 1900, was another who had a profound regard for the Book of Job and once said:

> "If a man die, shall he live again," 14:14—is the most important question ever asked. "But the path of the just is as the shining light, that shineth more and more unto the perfect day" Proverbs 4:18, is worth remembering in everyday life.

Professor Richard Moulton, the most outstanding literary scholar of the last century who gave the Christian world the religious classics of *The Modern Reader's Bible* and *The Literary Study of The Bible*, left us this estimation of Job:

> If a jury of persons well instructed in literature were impanelled to pronounce upon the question, What is the greatest poem in the world's great literature—While on

such a question, unanimity would be impossible. Yet I believe a large majority would give their verdict in favour of the Book of Job.

With its atmosphere of sin, sorrow, and silence, Job has been described as "The Matterhorn of the Old Testament"—a high estimation the ancient Jews agreed with when they placed the book in the third section of their canon. It is not a Jewish book and is completely silent regarding all Jewish ritual and worship. Job himself was a Gentile patriarch. Yet its sacred pages were studied in private that faith might be strengthened in God. The Jews do not read Job in the synagogue, as they do the Pentateuch and the Prophets. It is detached from sanctuary associations and kept at home for private reading. Like Proverbs, it is considered a people's book.

Professor W. G. Moorehead, the renowned Presbyterian theologian, wrote:

The Book of Job is one of the noblest poems in existence. The splendor of imagery which glows on every page; the personages introduced into it; the mysterious problems which it discusses; the action which sweeps through every emotion of the soul and strikes every chord of the human heart, invest the book with peculiar interest.

One could continue adding testimony after testimony from ancient and modern writers as to the intrinsic literary and spiritual value of Job. Unique among its kind, the book stands on its own merits. I maintain it towers alone, far above all the poetry in the world. My purpose, in this study, is to view the greatest production of Wisdom Literature upon its own merits and to prove that it is unequaled, whether we treat it as one of the supreme literary creations of the world or as one of the mightiest spiritual factors in the lives of multitudes throughout the ages.

In spite of its sublime, lofty language and poetic beauty, the Book of Job has received a good deal of adverse criticism and misunderstanding as to its historical verity. Some even question its spiritual influence. I see it as a part of the sacred canon. I deem it to be an integral part of God's infallible Word to man.

Part One

BACKGROUND FACTS ON THE BOOK OF JOB

1

Its Purpose for You

The pre-eminent purpose of the Book of Job is to answer the age-old question, Why does the just Ruler of the universe permit a good person to be afflicted? While we accept that what He permits must be for our profit, much about the subject of divine permission is difficult for us to understand.

The writer starts out to grapple with the ancient, yet modern, problem of the bafflements of Divine Providence and the mystery of human suffering. He searches for a straight answer to the never-ending question, Why do the righteous suffer? The questioner refuses to be put off with the proverbial philosophy of his day. Job knew that a person is happy who finds wisdom and secures understanding of the problem in question, but he asked where such wisdom could be found. Life is a serious business, but the secret of wisdom is deep and destiny is dark when the ways of God are past finding out. Yet Job's triumph over the problem assures us that by faith and endurance we can emerge from the black shadow into the bright sunshine.

This first of the Poetical Books was designed to give us a valuable insight into Satan's evil power. The Book of Job assures us that Satan has no ultimate power over those who abide in the shelter of the Divine Presence. The message is clear that Satan cannot go beyond the limit of divine command. Once he was given permission to try Job, Satan executed his commission with rapidity.

Blow after blow fell in quick succession. Finally, Job was robbed of all, except his trust in God.

Doesn't God often teach His children by stripping them of many things they cling to? It is only thus that He can enrich them spiritually. The purpose of the Lord, then, was not to create patience in Job, but to bring him to a penitent confession of his vileness. The withering blasts of adversity had their effect in this respect. This, then, is the key to the entire book. As for Job's three friends, they knew little of his character and of God's real object in dealing with His servant.

Professor Moorehead wrote of the design of the Book of Job as being of a threefold nature:

To refute the slander of Satan.

To discuss the question of human suffering, and particularly the suffering of the righteous.

To reveal Job to himself, and remove the self-righteousness which prevented the full measure of blessing which God had in store for him.

2

Its Antiquity

Job is a book without dates; hence it is neither characteristically dispensational nor historical. It is very ancient and carries the marks of antiquity. It may be equal in date with the Book of Genesis, and Job himself may have been contemporary with Isaac and Jacob. Job clearly lived before the age of man was shortened to "fourscore years," as in the day of Moses (see Ps. 90:10 KJV). If we accept the orthodox view of Job's association with the early Hebrew patriarchs, then his book has the peculiar distinction of being the oldest, as well as the grandest, book in the world. It goes back to the infancy of the human race when there was no Bible, no clear New Testament spiritual vision; yet there were men like Enoch, Noah, and Job who were borne along by the vision of the Almighty. The Book of Job bids us think of the dim ages of the past when humankind had nothing more than the few facts found in the first eight or nine chapters of Genesis, and it reveals what they thought about the universe and its God.

Job lived before sacrifices were confined to one altar, before the general apostasy of the people from the knowledge and worship of the true God to the idolatry of the worship of the sun and moon. The early patriarch lived at a time when God was known as *El Shaddai* (the Almighty One), a term occurring about thirty times in his book. During this period the knowledge of God was conveyed, not by inspired writing, but by tradition, hence, Job's constant appeal to it (see Job 5:1; 8:8; 15:18; 21:29). As there is no mention of deliverance from Egypt, or the giving of the Law, this book may have been written before the time of Moses. Some authorities suggest that there may be a reference to the drowning of Pharaoh and his host in Job 26:12: "He stirs up the sea with His power."

Walter Scott, who said in his *Bible Handbook* that the Book of Job was cast in the early patriarchal times between Abram and Moses, also affirmed that its scenes are laid in the Far East in the ancient country of Arabia, the only land in all antiquity that never bowed to the yoke of a foreign conqueror:

> Its customs, manners, and people are almost identical with the earliest ages of mankind; thousands of years have passed away, and yet the charming simplicity of patriarchal life, as exhibited in Abraham and Job, may be witnessed still in the ancient and interesting country, which has maintained its primitive character, while empires and kingdoms have flourished and fallen.

The fact remains that although millennia have passed since Job gathered his experiences together in the form we now have them, no advance has been made in respect to the beautiful language of the book bearing his name, or in the presentation of the solemn facts of human life. Possessing a character entirely its own, this book will remain precious to the hearts of God's people, who like Job pass through the fire of testing, or divinely permitted suffering, and come to experience the afterward of divine blessing and bounty. Job is an ageless book in that it mirrors the trials of saints in any age. Its philosophy is ever up-to-date.

3

Its Place in the Bible

In our Bible, the Book of Job occurs after the historical section of the Old Testament and is the first of the section known as the Poetical Books. In the Hebrew canon its position is somewhat different. It is placed after the Psalms, and sometimes after the Book of Proverbs. But I hold that it is fitly placed as the first of the Poetical Books, since the Psalms are devotional and Proverbs, practical.

The placement of the books in the English Bible is in keeping with their contents and development: Law: Genesis—Deuteronomy (five books); History: Joshua—Esther (twelve books); Poetry: Job—Song of Solomon (five books); and Prophecy: Isaiah—Malachi (seventeen books). The total is thirty-nine books.

4

Its Composition

Since much criticism, profitable and otherwise, has gathered around this ancient book we are considering, let me summarize the positions held by different scholars as to the nature of its composition.

Strictly Historical. The conservative approach is that everything recorded within the book actually happened. All the persons, human and angelic, referred to existed. All the experiences depicted did occur. This attitude was maintained by the Jews of early times and is the orthodox position today. As we shall prove, Job was a real person, and this book bearing his name is made up of real history.

Wholly Unhistorical. Many take a more liberal approach to Scripture, swing to the other extreme, and pronounce the Book of Job the lively creation of some poet's mind. Adherents to this approach see Job himself and other persons referred to as being imaginary or fictitious. Such critics contend that whoever wrote the book had an intimate and wide acquaintance with the world and thereby found some legends about a character called Job. The compiler drew them together and presented them in a poetical story form that has an undying message for all times.

Middle Position. Other scholars assume a central position between the two foregoing positions. They consider the Book of Job as a creation of some anonymous writer's own mind but that his poem rests upon historical tradition. It is a narrative founded by facts. Martin Luther, who held this view, wrote, "I hold the Book of Job to be real history; but that everything so happened and was so done, I do not believe. I think that some ingenious pious and learned man composed it as it is."

I have no hesitation in affirming that the Spirit-guided writer of the book has given us true history, not romance, even though the dialogue making up the bulk of it is poetical. There can be no doubt that Job was a real person, as the next chapter clearly proves.

5

Its Author

While doubt may be held as to the exact authorship of the book, there is no doubt as to its divine inspiration. The Jews have always retained it in their sacred canon, and I hold it to be a definite and specific part of the Holy Oracles of God. Who wrote the book? is a question more easily asked than answered. Its authorship has been a much disputed point. It has been attributed to various authors, such as Solomon, Isaiah, Ezra, Nehemiah, and Heman. Some authorities, like Bishop Lightfoot, connect its authorship with Elihu, basing their position upon the premise that he had the Spirit of prophecy which filled him with ideas and constrained him (see 32:8–18).

The Talmud, and several of the medieval rabbis, ascribed the book to Moses, who wrote it while in Midian. According to this belief, Moses wanted to encourage the hope that God would deliver his people from the oppression of Egypt. But I have no difficulty in believing that Job himself recorded, under divine inspiration, an account of his grievous experiences and that in later years such a diary came into the hands of Moses while he was an exile or fugitive in the land of Midian. As Job was "the greatest of all the people of the East" (1:3) and the places he mentioned were in close proximity to Midian, the possibility is that the record left by Job would be well known to Jethro, who in turn handed it to Moses. Thus the great lawgiver transcribed the record, adding the prologue and epilogue that describe Job's personal history. Then, because of the Jewish veneration of Moses, the book afterwards became a definite part of their sacred writings.

Whoever the author was, he is to be included among "the holy men of God [who] spoke as they were moved by the Holy Spirit" (2 Pet. 1:21). Paul claimed divine inspiration for the book in his quotation of Job 5:13, adding to the verse his usual formula of divine authority, "It is written" (1 Cor. 3:19).

Professor Moorehead, arguing that the question of its authorship can never be settled finally, found that the view that Moses wrote it appears very attractive. He went on to say that

> the anonymous character of the Book does not invalidate it. The authorship of Esther and of the Epistle to the Hebrews is unknown, yet their canonicity is not questioned. Of Hebrews, one of the Early Fathers is said to have exclaimed, "God alone knows who wrote it."

The contemporary Bible student does not have to know the author any more than a traveler needs to know the architect of an ancient cathedral. The traveler can appreciate the beauty of the structure; the student can gain spiritual insights from the ancient book.

6

Its Central Character

Seeing that the book carries the name of the patriarchal Job, we come to the question of whether Job was a real or fictitious character. Rabbi Maimonides, of the twelfth century, appears to have been the first to advance the theory of Job's nonexistence, but

> the extreme circumstantiality of details; the description of Job, of his family and friends, with their names and special designations, his country, his property, and many other points of the like nature, mark the history rather than fiction.

Did some clever genius of a writer plan this wonderful book and dream up the Job character whose experiences are portrayed in such detail? The best way to answer such a question is to summarize what Scripture has to say about Job.

THE FACTS OF HIS LIFE

The opening page of Job presents him as a rare specimen of a man, whose cup was full of earthly bliss. It gives us this brief, biographical sketch of this great man of the East: what he was in character—perfect and upright, feared God; what he had—much substance; and what he did—sanctified his own family.

25

That Job was no mythical personage, nor the circumstances recounted merely imaginary, nor the book only a parable, as some suppose, is proven by the precise details given of the patriarch's history. The mention of his name and the place where he lived reveal that the biographer meant to affirm that there was, in fact, such a man as Job. His abode was in the land of Uz (1:1). His name was Job (1:1).

The significance of such a name is not easy to determine. Walter Scott said it means "treated with hostility," and that such a name, occurring some sixty times in Scripture, pictured "self and human righteousness withered up by the hand and in the presence of God." Other interpretations of his name are given as "one who is hated, counted as an enemy," "one who grieves or groans" (an indication of the sorrow he carried in his name as a check to joy over his prosperity), and "to love, desire" (a reference to the joy of his parents over his welcome birth). Yet he came to curse the day of his birth!

Job's character was "blameless and upright" (1:1), and he "feared God and shunned evil" (1:1). These precise facts undoubtedly prove that Job existed and that he was known by others as a man with these godly traits of character.

Of his family we learn that he had "seven sons and three daughters" (1:2). His wife evidently did not share her husband's attitude toward his great grief and loss when she urged him to "curse God and die." How magnificent was Job's rebuke! (See 2:9–10.)

His possessions consisted of "seven thousand sheep, three thousand camels, five hundred yoke of oxen, five hundred female donkeys, and a very large household" (1:3). Such original greatness and substance have little to do with the main line of the book. These particular details are overdone and altogether unnecessary if Job were only a fictitious character. His wealth, wisdom, and worth earned him the reputation of being "the greatest of all the people of the East" (1:3).

His friends were "Eliphaz the Temanite, Bildad the Shuhite, and Zophar the Naamathite" (2:11). Eliphaz and Bildad each addressed Job three times and Zophar twice. Later on we will more fully study Job's "three friends." Suffice it to say at this point that all three are associated with a local habitation and given a specific name. These details would not have been necessary if Job were only an imaginary person. Job's anguish was that of having his familiar friends forsake him.

His foes were "the Sabeans" (1:15), "the Chaldeans" (1:17), and Satan. If Job is only a parable, it would have been truer to the context to use the term "robbers" of these foes. Also the patriarch's contact with his archfoe Satan, who charged Job with false accusations, breathes the air of reality.

Job's age was 210. What we know of Job's age places him among the ancient men who were known for their longevity. When he "died, old and full of days" (42:17), he was over 200 years old; this age agrees with those who lived between Peleg, who died at the age of 239, and Abraham, who was 175 years of age when he died (see Gen. 11:19; 25:7). The record tells us that Job lived 140 years after his double blessing which, if it included length of years, would make his age 210 (70 + 140 = 210). With the length of life gradually decreasing, we can place Job between the Deluge and the call of Abraham, or between Genesis 11 and 12—an additional proof that God never left the ancient world without a witness. Of his sufferings, his integrity, and his reward we shall have more to say in succeeding pages.

Suffice it to say that the Septuagint places Job "fifth from Abraham." E. W. Bullinger, the renowned Hebrew and Greek scholar, connected Job with the Job of Genesis 46:13, thus proving him to be a son of Issachar. Then this expositor stated that it was possible for Job to have been alive when Moses was a man of fifty-five, and therefore quite simple for him to have been an eyewitness to all that happened to Job in Midian, seeing that he had come hither with Issachar.

PROOFS OF HIS REALITY

In addition to the foregoing proofs of Job's reality as a person, we have the inclusive evidence of God, and of sacred writers, proving as Ewald expressed it, "An entire invention, either of a person or of a history is a thing unknown in the earliest antiquity." The general rule of ancient literature, and of Scripture, was to make use of actual events and persons.

1. *Divine Witness.* Six times God designated Job as "My servant" (1:8; 2:3; 42:7–8), and every reverent mind rests here. It would be unlike and unworthy of God to speak thus of one who did not actually exist.

2. *Prophetic Witness.* The prophet Ezekiel associated Job with Noah and Daniel: "These three men, Noah, Daniel, and Job" (Ezek. 14:14). He referred to Job in such a way as to make his identity as real as the other two servants of God. If Noah and Daniel were real persons, so was Job, whose righteous character availed on behalf of others.

3. *Apostolic Witness.* Apart from Paul's quotation from Eliphaz's first discourse (Job 5:13 found in 1 Cor. 3:19), we have the evidence of James as to Job's existence: "You have heard of the perseverance of Job and seen the end intended by the Lord—that the Lord is very compassionate and merciful" (James 5:11). The virtue of "per-

severance" can only be related to living beings. Further, God does not have dealings with imaginary characters. The reference would be "wholly without point, and an impeachment of the Apostle's inspiration if Job were mythical."

Thus I contend that Job existed and that his character and story are truly portrayed in the book bearing his name.

7

Its Setting in Time

Scholars disagree as to the time line of the Book of Job. They place it in different periods ranging from the age before Moses right down to Solomon's time. Some hold a still later date because its perfection of wisdom is parallel with that of the Wisdom Literature of Solomon. But accepting, as I do, that Job described the patriarchal age, or the time of Abraham, Isaac, and Jacob, I will cite evidence in support of this view.

THE OMISSION OF ISRAEL

A reading of Job makes it clearly evident that it is unconnected with God's covenant people, the Jews, with whom so much of the Old Testament is associated. The book occupies an isolated position, in that it was written by one outside the Israelite nation. There are no allusions to the Mosaic Law or to the deliverance of the Israelites and their journey to Canaan, which fill the works of other sacred writers. Historical references of any directness are usually connected with the great events of the ancient, patriarchal world.

ANCIENT CUSTOMS

Several features given of ancient customs from the scope of the book indicate that it is of great antiquity—some say the oldest book in the world.

1. *The Kesita.* The use of this term meaning "piece of silver" (42:11) connects the Book of Job with early patriarchal times. Jacob bought a parcel of ground with "one hundred pieces of money" (Gen. 33:19).

2. *The Writing.* The writing mentioned "on a rock with an iron pen and lead" (Job 19:24) is the most ancient kind of recordkeeping that is known. The *book* of 19:23 is the *rock* of 19:24. Job desired his words to be hewn out in indelible characters upon the rock, and then filled in with lead. Thus they would be made imperishable. The passage has been translated thus:

> Oh, that my words were written!
> Oh, that they were inscribed in a book!
> That they were engraved on a rock
> With an iron pen and lead, forever!

3. *The Musical Instruments.* Reference to instruments of music, tambourine or timbrel, harp, and flute or organ (see Job 21:12), was to the simple instruments used in primitive times soon after the commencement of the human race. Jubal was the father of all that handle the harp and the flute (see Gen. 4:21).

4. *The Representation of Wealth.* Like the forefathers of Israel, Job was described as rich in cattle and herds. At that period in history, cattle were riches. The animal possessions of Job were the same type as those constituting Abraham's wealth (see Gen. 12:16).

5. *The Sacrificial Worship.* The religion of Job was one of sacrifices, but without any official priest to prepare and offer them, as in Israel's day. In patriarchal times, the head of the family acted as priest and offered sacrifices to God for the household. The "burnt offerings" referred to in Job 1:5 are not to be confused with the more developed ritual God later prescribed for Israel.

It was an offering similar to that of Abel (see Gen. 4:4), which continued from his day to be observed.

Note that the only form of idolatry alluded to in the Book of Job was that which is found in the earliest records of the human race. The worship or adoration of heavenly bodies, such as the sun and moon or heavenly hosts, was condemned at an early time (see Deut. 4:19).

6. *The Inheritance.* The daughters of Job were spoken of as receiving an inheritance among their brethren, a custom more fully recognized in later years.

7. *The Language.* Fausset observed that "the simpler and less artificial forms of Poetry that prevail in Job, are a mark of an early age." The Orientals in ancient times preserved their sentiments in a terse, proverbial, poetic form known as *Mashal,* or *Maschil* (Instruction Psalm), to which Job's poetry is akin.

8

Its Unique Features

As the Book of Job is one of the most remarkable books ever written, one can expect many of its features and peculiarities to be of an illuminative character. Consider several of them, and meditate on their truths.

Key Verse. The whole point of the book is found in the question asked by Satan, "Does Job fear God for nothing?" (1:9). It means, "Does Job worship the Lord for nothing?" Satan's accusation was that Job served God, not because he had any deep reverence for Him, but simply because it *paid* him to be religious. Thus he was guilty of ulterior motives. But such an accusation defamed both God's character and Job's, and so the patriarch found himself in the crucible of trial. He had to prove to Satan that as God's servant he was not two-faced or a hypocrite, and he did not serve God simply for the prospect of material prosperity.

God permitted Job to be stripped completely. According to Satan's contention, Job would turn from God and curse Him when there was nothing to trust God for. But Job clung to God with a naked faith, even though he could not understand God's dealings with him. Grace was his to trust God even when he could not trace Him. Job, ignorant of Satan's false accusation, maintained his way before God and triumphantly declared, "Though He slay me, yet will I trust Him" (13:15).

Key Thought. This can readily be adduced from the key verse. Suffering that Satan inflicts is permitted by

God for ends that glorify Him. Job's experience was cited as an illustration that trial and loss often overtake God's children, not because they have sinned and deserved chastisement, but as a means of spiritual edification and growth (see Heb. 12:5–12). God testified to Job's holiness in no uncertain terms, "There is none like him on the earth, a blameless and upright man, one who fears God and shuns evil" (Job 1:8).

Yet see how God allowed him to suffer! Does he not stand out as a type of Jesus Who was made perfect through suffering? That Job's adversity brought him to a fuller revelation of his need of God is evident from the last chapter of his book. If we can find no cause for the suffering God is presently allowing, may we commit our way unto Him in the calm assurance that He is working out His own beneficent purpose.

Key Words. Professor Moorehead suggested that *chastisement* is the key word of Job and cited 34:31–32. But I cannot limit myself to one. I find several repeated words carrying key thoughts. For instance, *righteous* and its equivalents occur twenty-two times; *teach*, fifteen times; *justification*, fourteen times; *curse*, ten times; *clean*, or its equivalent, nine times; *trust*, nine times; *prayer*, eight times; and *words*, thirty-eight times, the importance of which is emphasized later on in this study.

The lover of Scripture will find a storehouse of devotional material in such a word study. For example, let us take the eight references to prayer, and note the nature, scope, and profit of such a privilege:

The first reference (8:5) could be taken as the basic verse.

The second reference (15:4) speaks of restrained prayer, the context providing causes for such restraint.

The third reference (16:17) reminds us of purity of motive in prayer.

The fourth reference (21:15) emphasizes useless, empty prayer.

The fifth reference (22:27) extols profitable prayer.

The sixth reference (33:26) reveals the blessedness of prayer.

The seventh reference (42:8) describes intercessory prayer.

The eighth reference (42:10) gives us emancipating prayer.

Other suggestive words like *mediator* (*daysman* in KJV), *ransom*, and *Redeemer* demand the attention of the student of Job's marvelous book. The usage "the sons of God" (1:6), rendered in some translations as "the angels of God" and referred to at the Creation in 38:7, introduces one to the fascinating study of angels, as my volume on *The Unseen Army* proves.

PECULIAR CUSTOMS

Whoever the writer of this book was, he was a man familiar with the customs and ways of his time. The following are a few of them.

"Skin for skin" (2:4). In all probability this was a common proverb that Satan used against Job. The phrase may be associated with the time when a trade was conducted by barter or exchange of goods. Skins of animals, being a most valuable commodity, were used in some way to represent property. Satan's use of the phrase implied that Job was willing to part with anything in order to save his own life.

"Sprinkled dust" (2:11–12). The peculiar custom is one of extreme antiquity and was a sign of intense grief. In the East, mourners would take up a handful of dust and scatter it over their heads or throw it heavenward.

"A runner" (9:25). Postal delivery in Job's land was extremely slow, camels or horses being used to carry couriers with written or oral messages. Specific paces were allowed for each beast or runner, and at the end of a given pace, a fresh beast or runner was ready to complete the journey without halting. Job effectively used this ancient mode of transmitting messages to illustrate the brevity of life.

"Swift ships" (9:26). A possible translation of the Hebrew is "ships of desire" or "ships of Eber." Alacrity of movement is also implied in the eagle hastening to its prey, found in the last part of verse 26 and also in the phrase, "swifter than a runner." "Ships of Eber" was a proper name of a particular kind of boat in use on the Nile and suggests Job's acquaintance with Egypt. Because of their construction, boats moved faster than most kinds of land travel. A scourge overtook Job suddenly and swiftly.

"Cover my blood" (16:18). There may be an allusion here to a very old belief that the blood of one unjustly slain remained in the earth. One reference to such an idea can be traced to Genesis 4:10 and confirms the antiquity of the Book of Job. The phrase, as used by the patriarch, implied that it was his desire that the witness of his inexplicable sufferings should not be hidden.

"Their tokens" (21:29 KJV). The travelers referred to were those who went from one place to another in caravans, which possibly were the first mode of travel. The "tokens" carried were simply the knowledge of persons or events a traveler would gather on his journey and then would repeat to friends when he halted. As a means of carrying news, such a method of oral repetition would be most acceptable.

"One to hear me" (31:35). My free rendering of this portion reads:

Oh, that I had one to hear me!
Lo, here is my signature, let the Almighty answer me;
And that I had the indictment which mine adversary
    hath written.

There may be an allusion here to the writing out of law cases which existed early in Egypt. What Job meant by his use of such law language was that he was ready to put his signature to his case, defend his innocence, and then display abroad his pride of defense.

We cannot do better, as we pass from some of the peculiar features of the book before us, than to point out that it is a book of striking contrasts. Think of these illustrations!

The first chapter recites Job's great wealth; the second chapter, his utter destitution. The prince became a pauper.

Then God and Satan were brought together in a solemn wager regarding Job's sincerity. God, the source of all that is pure, holy, and just, bargained with Satan, the source of all that is hateful, iniquitous, and despicable.

Further, we have the contrast of view as represented in the dialogue between Job and his friends. The latter contended that Job was suffering because he was sinful. On the other hand, Job himself protested his innocence and declared that the righteous as well as the sinful are afflicted by God.

Contemplate the paradox of Job's character. At the beginning of the book we are told that he was "blameless and upright" and also "shunned evil." He even called himself blameless. Later Job confessed, "Behold, I am vile" (40:4) and "I abhor myself and repent in dust and ashes" (42:6). Such a confession seemed essential in the presence of a thrice-holy God.

9

Its Coverage of the Sciences

My study of the ancient Book of Job has led me to conclude that its range of observation, reflection, and experience is probably larger than that of any other book in the Bible or of any other ancient book. If this record of Job's experiences formed the first complete book ever written, then even in that remote age the patriarch and his adversaries had a remarkable scope of knowledge.

The sciences touched upon in this book of antiquity disprove the tenets of the evolutionists. Their views have gained much ground in recent years, but I think they oppose the biblical view of the creation of human beings. In short, the theory of evolution is this: Humans, and all things, have gradually developed, passing from lower forms to higher forms. The theory claims that humans were not brought into being by one specific, divine creative act but came into existence as the result of a slow process of evolution. Commencing as protoplasm, or a small, shapeless, homogeneous lump of matter similar to the jellyfish we see at the seashore, life progressed slowly. From a low form of life to a higher form, it continued until the stage of the ape was reached. This animal more closely resembles the human being than any other.

The difficulty confronting the evolutionists, however, is the missing link. The form of life between the ape and man has never been found. Darwin, one of the most renowned evolutionists, had to confess, "The great break in the organic chain between man and his nearest allies cannot be bridged over by any extinct, or living species."

The question I ask of those who believe we descended from apes is this: Why do apes not continue to evolve? Needless to say, I utterly reject this modern rationalistic way of explaining the existence of humans. Accepting as I do the Almightiness of God, I see no reason why He was not able, in a moment of time, to create man out of a few particles of dust, as the Bible says He did.

The Book of Job does far more than disprove a modern scientific theory. The following sciences I have chosen to discuss all have the same ending, namely, "ology," a suffix coming from the word *logos*, which means "a treatise, composition, study, or discourse of any given subject."

COSMOLOGY

The term *cosmos* is the Greek word for "universe." The word signifies "orderly" or "systematic." *Cosmology* is related to the structure and nature of the universe.

Modern scientific minds are perplexed by the fact that men of such a remote age as Job's had such an accurate conception of the universe, a conception discredited by some scientists, yet returned to as being most accurate. Think of the language of wonderful, poetic beauty, yet of scientific accuracy, used to describe the composition of our globe with divine power (26:1–14). How striking is verse 7:

He stretches out the north over empty space;
He hangs the earth on nothing.

An old idea was that the universe was supported by pillars of some sort, a theory common in mythology. Legend told of a powerful giant named Atlas who bore the heavens on his shoulders. Now the name *atlas* is used to denote a book of maps, the first vertebra of the neck, and a mountain range in Africa.

But modern scientific knowledge has discovered that in some mysterious way the earth is entirely unsupported, and Job, many millennia ago, declared it was so when he wrote that "God hangs the earth on nothing." What a sublime picture of God's masterly constructed and beautifully created universe we have as we string all the scientific passages in Job together!

Thick clouds cover Him, so that He cannot see,
And He walks above the circle of heaven (22:14).

He covers His hands with lightning,
And commands it to strike (36:32).

By the breath of God ice is given,
And the broad waters are frozen (37:10).

Study chapters 37, 38, and 39. They afford marvelous evidences of God's creative power and will leave you in adoring wonder. While the Bible does not claim to be a scientific treatise but a revelation of God's redemptive purpose, its scientific accuracy cannot be refuted or superseded. The Book of Job invites the honest scientific mind to examine all it reveals of the creation and content of the marvelous world around us.

GEOLOGY

This science deals with the history and development of the earth's crust. The term comes from *geo*, the Greek term for "earth." The realm of *geology* is one in which evolutionists have delighted to speculate, their general theory being that the earth gradually evolved from a starting point billions of years ago. But the Bible, as a divine revelation, is more specific. Scripture affirms quite plainly, "God created the heavens and the earth." Even in Job's day, people had a true conception of how the earth came into being.

> He shakes the earth out of its place, and . . .
> He alone spreads out the heavens (9:6,8).

> He drew a circular horizon on the face of the waters,
> At the boundary of light and darkness (26:10).

> As for the earth . . . underneath it is turned up as by fire (28:5).

Job's conception of earth's creation corresponds with the opening sentence of the Bible; that is, it was not evolved by its own inherent power but came into being by the specific, creative act of God. Accepting the omnipotence of God as I do, I see no reason why He could not fashion the heavens and the earth. Some geologists argue that the age of the earth can be proved to be far older than the calculated period of Bible history, and therefore the Bible is wrong. But, as eminent Bible scholars have pointed out, a great cataclysm occurred between Genesis 1:1 and 1:2. The first asserts a fact, "In the beginning God created the heavens and the earth," while the next verse speaks of a disordered creation, "The earth was without form, and void." Between these two verses, we can allow the geologist the enormous ages he demands, but what happened to mar God's original creation is another matter. The conservative explanation of the drastic change is that it was a divine judgment resulting from Satan's desire to be a creative god, and of his consequent expulsion from the divine abode (see Ezek. 28:12–15; Is. 14:9–14). When with Job we can confess before God, "I know that You can do everything" (42:2), then we have no doubt about His power to create the earth out of nothing.

MINERALOGY

If one splits the word *mineralogy* in two, the first half, *miner,* implies the thought of mining or digging in the earth to discover its valuable substances. Minerals are inorganic substances found within or upon the earth. The craft of the miner supplied Job with illustrations for his thoughts. He talked about the miserable person's seeking death "more than hidden treasures" (3:21). That he was familiar with mining operations and the achievement of early engineering is evident from his description of the treasures the earth yields to search (see 28:1–3).

Reading through this ancient Book of Job, one is amazed at the many products of the earth the patriarch knew about. Chapter 28 is remarkable for the catalogue of the precious things of the earth. Consider the following references from that and other chapters: gold and silver (3:15; 28:1,17,19); copper (28:2; brass, KJV); brimstone (18:15); iron (20:24; 28:2); bronze (20:24; steel, KJV); oil (24:11; 29:6); sapphires (28:6,16); onyx (28:16); jewels (28:17); crystal (28:17); and rubies and topaz (28:18–19). In a unique way Job used these valuable products of the earth, placed there by the hand of God, to illustrate spiritual and moral truths. For instance, Job said, "The price of wisdom is above rubies" (28:18).

METEOROLOGY

Today, weather predictions come from our highly developed meteorological centers. We are accustomed to the daily reports we receive of weather conditions. *Meteorology* is the science dealing with the atmosphere and the air. It is related to the appearance of rain, clouds, storms, thunder, lightning, climate, and mist. The Greek root words are *meta* (beyond) and *eōra* (anything suspended). Thus meteorology deals with all that is suspended or above the earth.

Job is outstanding among the books of the Bible in its record of atmospheric conditions and of their spiritual application. Light and darkness, snow and hail, storms, rain, dew, ice and frost, sunshine and clouds are referred to in a way that has never been excelled. The following passages prove the Book of Job to be one of the world's meteorological masterpieces: 1:16,19; 5:10; 7:9; 8:2; 12:15; 15:2,15; 24:8,19; 26; 27:21; 28:26; 29:19; 36:27; 37; 38.

One specific scientific aspect I would draw attention to, namely, "the balance of clouds" (37:16). Here you read of this ancient man expressing the atmospheric laws bearing upon the adjustment of vapors and gases with remarkable exactitude. He seemed to know laws that form the foundation of all scientific knowledge built upon research. How did Job come by all this knowledge of the compositon and workings of the universe? The only answer is that the God Who created the heavens and earth revealed to Job all the secrets of the world He brought into being by His fiat.

ASTRONOMY

The science of the stars also occupies a large place in this wonderful book. The term *astronomy* is derived from the word *astron* (a star). Job's astronomical references reveal not only a familiarity with the heavenly bodies, but an exact knowledge of their appearances and phenomena. The evolutionist would have us believe that people in that distant age were intellectually dwarfed but later generations gradually developed. Yet astronomers of our so-called advanced age cannot improve upon the names and salient features of the heavenly bodies handed down from Job. Think of these facts, written some six thousand years ago:

He made the Bear, Orion, and the Pleiades,
And the chambers of the south (9:9; see also Amos 5:8).

Can you bind the cluster of the Pleiades [or the seven stars],
Or loose the belt of Orion? (38:31).

Can you bring out Mazzaroth in its season?
Or can you guide the Great Bear with its cubs?
Do you know the ordinances of the heavens? (38:32–33).

Where were you when I laid the foundations of the earth? . . .
When the morning stars sang together . . . ? (38:4,7).

Is not God in the height of heaven?
And see the highest stars, how lofty they are! (22:12).

How then can man be righteous before God? . . .
If even the moon does not shine,
And the stars are not pure in His sight . . . ? (25:4–5).

Astronomy differs from astrology. The present-day, widespread, absorbing interest in astrology, the belief that stars and planets have an influence on human lives, had no part in Job's thinking. Our times are in no way bound up in the stars we are supposed to be born under, but only in the hands of Him Who made the stars. The Book of Genesis affirms that God "made the stars also" (1:16). Job confirmed such a divine creation when he wrote, "By His Spirit He adorned the heavens;/His hand pierced the fleeing serpent [name of a prominent star]" (26:13). The worship of the heavenly luminaries is the only form of idolatry mentioned in Job. It was, without question, the most ancient idolatrous practice (see Job 31:26–28).

ZOOLOGY

It is from the Greek word *zōon* (animal) that we have the terms *zoo* and *zoology*, both of which are connected with all kinds of animals and birds. Another striking feature of Job is the way animals, reptiles, birds, and beasts of all description fill its pages. You will find superb descriptions of their outstanding features; for example, what can compare with the description given of the famous war-horse (see 39:19-25)?

Here is a compilation of God's creatures passing before us in review: sheep, camels, oxen, and asses (1:3); deer and goats (39:1); bulls and cows (21:10); lions (4:10); horses (39:19); wild ox (39:9; unicorn, KJV); behemoth (40:15); dogs (30:1); sea serpent (7:12; whale, KJV); leviathan (41:1); ravens, hawks, eagles (38:41; 39:26; 9:26); jackals and ostriches (30:29; dragons and owls, KJV); moths (4:19); spiders (8:14); cobras (20:14; asps, KJV); worms (17:14); and locusts (39:20; grasshoppers, KJV).

Related to the science of zoology is *oology,* from the Greek word *óon* (an egg). Lovers of birds and their eggs can also find these interesting features in Job to think on:

Let them try to answer the question of 6:6, "Is there any taste in the white of an egg?"

Let them try to understand the method of the ostrich and her eggs (39:13–15).

Let them try to comprehend why the eagle places her eggs where she does (39:27).

What a marvelous coverage of the zoological world Job gives us! Truly, the accuracy of insight, definiteness of knowledge, and precision of observation are unique in a book of so ancient a date!

PHYTOLOGY

Phyton is the Greek word for "plant"; thus *phytology* is the science that brings us to botanical references found in the Book of Job. It is evident from these and other passages related to trees and flowers that the patriarch was a profound lover of Nature. How apt was his spiritual application of all he saw around him!

Can the papyrus grow up without a marsh?
Can reeds flourish without water?
While it is yet green and not cut down,
It withers before any other plant.
So are the paths of all who forget God (8:11–13).

Man . . . comes forth like a flower and fades away (14:1–2).

The flame will dry out his branches . . . .
And his branch will not be green.

He will shake off his unripe grape like a vine,
And cast off his blossom like an olive tree (15:30–33).

If I have eaten its fruit without money . . . .
Then let thistles grow instead of wheat,
And weeds instead of barley (31:39,40).

In this most picturesque fashion Job protested his integrity. He not only "feared God and shunned evil" (1:1), but he manifested sincere, upright, and consistent conduct.

DENDROLOGY

Allied to the plants Job mentioned is the science of trees. *Dendron*, the Greek word for "tree," brings us to the science dealing with the natural history of trees. A somewhat perplexing feature of the Book of Job is the variety of similes drawn from Nature the patriarch uses. There are all the conditions of a tropical or semitropical climate combined with those of an almost arctic rigor—those belonging to a well-watered land and those of a barren desert. Thus we have the cedar alongside the willow and the juniper. Here, again, we see how Job was gifted in using the natural world as a parable of the spiritual realm.

For there is hope for a tree,
If it is cut down, that it will sprout again,
And that its tender shoots will not cease.
Though its root may grow old in the earth,
And its stump may die in the ground,
Yet at the scent of water it will bud
And bring forth branches like a plant.
If a man dies, shall he live again? (14:7–9,14).

Men younger than I . . . pluck mallow by the bushes,
And broom tree roots for their food.
Among the bushes they brayed,
Under the nettles they nestled.
They were sons of fools (30:1,4,7–8).

He [behemoth] moves his tail like a cedar . . .
He lies under the lotus trees,
In a covert of reeds and marsh.
The lotus trees cover him with their shade;
The willows by the brook surround him (40:17,21–22).

ETYMOLOGY

We now come to the science dealing with the original signification of words and names. *Etymos* is the Greek word for "true." In ancient times, names were carefully chosen, when not divinely given, and were related to the nature and character of the recipients. I have found the meaning of Bible names to be a fascinating and fruitful study. Because of my interest in names I have written several books: *All the Men of the Bible*, *All the Women of the Bible*, and *All the Divine Names and Titles in the Bible*.

Job (1:1) and *Satan* (1:6). Job's name, when rightly understood, gives a clue to the problem set forth in the book bearing that name. The most acceptable interpretation of *Job* is "the assaulted or attacked or afflicted one." The name comes from the same root as "hated" or "was an enemy." Job, because of his integrity, became an enemy of Satan; hence Satan's hatred toward Job and his cruel accusations regarding his character. *Satan* means "adversary." He accused Job, and he has ever been the adversary of God and man.

Job's Daughters: *Jemimah*, *Keziah*, and *Keren-Happuch*

(42:14). The names given by Job to his three daughters after his restoration and justification by God describe their personal characteristics.

Jemimah. This female name signifies "as fair as the day." Possibly, since she was the first of Job's ten children, he gave her the name to commemorate his re-emergence into a bright and sunny day from the dark night of anguish through which he had passed.

Keziah. To his second daughter, Job gave a name meaning "cassia," and it is so translated in Psalm 45:8. Cassia was a very fragrant bark that was much prized by the ancients. Thus, because of the pleasantness and value of its perfume, Job called his daughter by its name. He desired her to be pleasant and precious as cassia. As there were no women so fair as Job's daughters in all the land, evidently they were all most attractive.

Keren-Happuch. This long, strange name is highly interesting. It is connected with a custom of great antiquity. It means "a horn or vessel for containing paint" that was used for coloring the eyes—a custom many modern women use to excess. Eastern women of Job's day were in the habit of painting the upper part of their eyelids with a particular kind of paint, so that a black edge formed about them, thereby making them appear larger. This adornment was looked upon as a sign of personal charm or beauty. For such, the women had little horns or containers to hold the paint, and these can be seen in museums today.

Doubtless Job, recognizing and appreciating the personal beauty and attractiveness of his third daughter, gave her a name marking her out as one of the most handsome women of her day. Paint, or powder, used by Oriental women may have added luster to the eye, but

Job desired his daughter's character to be as beautiful as her countenance.

Early names, then, were associated with personal traits or experiences of those bearing such names. I will deal with the significance of the names of Job's friends as we come to the dramatic content of his book.

TERMINOLOGY

One meaning of the word *term* is a "sentence in which a thought is expressed, or a word or phrase considered to be the same, or symbol of something." Even the most casual reader of the Book of Job must be aware that it is loaded with gems of truth and pearls of wisdom. Job and his friends certainly knew how to pack tremendous thoughts in short, crisp sentences. The masterly, proper way in which the speakers in the dialogue that forms the bulk of the book were able to set forth their convictions and contentions has never been surpassed. In spite of their antiquity, many of the apt, wise terms, or figures of speech, still command universal admiration. What intelligence and ability so many of its terse sayings reveal! Space forbids a full catalogue of all its pungent paragraphs, but here are some to prove my point.

Does Job fear God for nothing? (1:9).

Curse God and die! (2:9).

You shall come to the grave at a full age,
As a sheaf of grain ripens in its season (5:26).

My days are swifter than a weaver's shuttle . . . (7:6).

Oh, that one might plead for a man with God,
As a man pleads for his neighbor! (16:21).

My brethren have dealt deceitfully like a brook (6:15).

C. J. Ellicott commented that "This is one of the most celebrated similes in the book, and carries us to life in the desert, where the wadys, so mighty and torrent-like in the winter, are insignificant streams or fail altogether in summer." The metaphor of the brook occurs in Job's reply to Eliphaz in which he expressed the despair of a man who had been deprived of sympathy when and where he had hoped to find it.

Further, what can compare with figures such as "words like a strong wind" (8:2) and the fashioning of life as "curdle me like cheese" (10:10)? We are attracted to the likening of the brevity of life to a "weaver's shuttle" (7:6).

ETHNOLOGY

We come to the science concerning nations and races. *Ethnology* comes from *ethnos* (nation). For those who are interested in ethnological aspects of Scripture, the Book of Job is a valuable handbook regarding those earliest races inhabiting the earth. Several races, along with racial characteristics, are mentioned:

The Sabeans (1:15). The narrator makes it clear that these were a race of people who lived by plunder and pillage.

The Chaldeans (1:17). These were a people similar in their ways and habits to the Sabeans.

The Arabians (6:19). A people who lived and traveled in caravans, the Arabians were a fascinating race, having a colorful history.

The People (24:4–12; 30:1–8). Doubtless these were aboriginal races living an outcast life, dwelling in caves, finding their substance in the wilderness, and adopting customs and manners all their own.

The Lord of all Nations. The One Who "makes nations great, and destroys them" (12:23) is often spoken of as the Ruler over all races.

ANTHROPOLOGY

Here we have the science of man, dealing with human history in the broadest sense. The term is from the Greek *anthropos* (man). The evolutionist does not take kindly to Job, for this book gives the lie to his theory as to the origin of man. This ancient volume is unique in that it gives us a complete history of man: his direct creation; his power to please the God Who created him; his proneness to trial and suffering; his power of endurance; his greatness; and his death. Condemned and criticized though it is, this remarkable book acts as a divine commentary on the whole of man from his proverbial cradle to the grave.

Let us take one aspect only of the subject of man, namely, his creation. The evolutionist discredits the record of Genesis that man was created by God and affirms that he gradually evolved from a jellyfish form through billions of years until he became a man. But Elihu, who was acquainted with the facts of the Creation as given in Genesis 1–2, declared:

> The Spirit of God hath made me,
> And the breath of the Almighty gives me life (Job 33:4).

Such a specific statement refutes the contention of the evolutionist that man evolved from lower forms of life and from fish and beast. Elihu had no doubt, just as I have none, that man represents a definite, divine creation. The nobility of man is degraded by affirming that he came from a monkey, not that I have anything against monkeys with their humanlike actions. But human beings did not evolve; they were created.

ETHOLOGY

A fact that none can dispute is the high standard of morals and ethical living found in such a book of great antiquity. The term above is from *ethos* (custom) and gives us the word *ethics*. *Ethology*, then, is the science relating to the character of man.

Evolution teaches that humans were very immature in the dim ages of the past but that they have come through a long, gradual process to their present state of morality. As man began to evolve, he became shaped more like a man, grew in love, and in the upper progress of his career became more responsible for his actions.

But I hold that when God created man out of a few particles of dust in a moment of time, He created him perfect. It was only after sin came into his life that his character became warped.

Where can you find a higher standard of ethics than that forming chapter 29! One would think Job had studied the Sermon on the Mount beforehand! Read this magnificent chapter slowly. What equity to servants! What tenderness to the poor! What graciousness to the afflicted! What purity of morals! What genial fatherliness! Here there is a stately dignity—an air of innate refinement marking Job as one of Nature's gentle men, one whom the sophistication of our twentieth-century conceit would neither dare to pity nor to patronize. What a different society ours would be if only our legislators, educators, and employers sought to live out the principles by which the model man Job lived!

Further, what can equal the superb humility of Elihu (32:4–6), or the largeheartedness of Job as well as the honesty of the friends in acknowledgment of their wrongs (42:9–10)? If we desire to learn manners, practice morality, and live ethically, all we have to do is to emulate the striking example of Job who was "perfect and upright," even in God's estimation.

SOCIOLOGY

With the awakened social conscience of our day, we read a great deal about the science of sociology, which deals with man as a social being. The study is related to the origin and development of human society, especially the social institutions. The term *sociology* is from the Latin *socius* (companion). Well, what has Job to say about the manners and customs of man as a social being? Sociologists could not do better than study this book for an answer to some problems they face today.

What mutual, social happiness existed within Job's family! What a beautiful home life and social pleasures they had! (See 1:1–5.) Then, as friendship is one of the foundations of our true, social well-being, think of the three friends who came to comfort Job and of the companionship they exhibited (see 2:11–13). Are not the weakness, coldness, and hollowness of modern society exposed by the way in which Job's brothers, sisters, and friends came to console him in the midst of disasters overtaking him and to make liberal gifts to the impoverished man? (See 42:11.) Social life would be purer, godlier, and richer if only our homes and friendships were modeled after what this old-time book records.

PSYCHOLOGY

The study of the human mind is very much to the fore in educational circles today. *Psychology*, the science which classifies and analyzes the phenomena or varying states and workings of the human mind, is from the Greek term *psyche* (soul). To all students of this branch of investigation the Book of Job offers a wide field. The actions and mood of the mind, from elation to depression, are exhibited through the effects of extreme suffering upon Job. The speeches of his three friends and his answers to them convince me that, although these characters lived thousands of years ago, they knew a good deal regarding the psychological laws governing the mind. Truly, as Solomon, a great psychologist in his way, expressed it, "There is nothing new under the sun" (Eccl. 1:9). If man would *know* himself, all he has to do is to study Bible characters, noting the differing moods and movements of their minds.

CRIMINOLOGY

It may surprise you to learn that the science dealing with crime and criminals also finds a place in this ancient Book of Job. Evidently, robbery was cleverly practiced in the patriarch's day. With the help of a good concordance and a reliable commentary, you can trace the disguises used by old-time robbers and criminals to achieve their ends. Here are some of the crime references in Job:

The tents of robbers prosper (12:6).

There are those who rebel against the light . . . .
The murderer rises with the light;
He kills the poor and needy;
And in the night he is like a thief (24:13–14).

The eye of the adulterer waits for the twilight,
Saying, "No eye will see me";
And he disguises his face (24:15).

He preys on the barren who do not bear,
And does no good for the widow (24:21).

These and other references to the evil springing from
the human heart prove that sin is as old as the world
and came upon it as the result of the fall of its first inhabitants.

PATHOLOGY

As a book of suffering, Job is without equal. This is
why it remains precious to God's suffering saints. *Pathos*
is the Greek word for "suffering." *Pathology* is the science dealing with the nature, causes, and remedies of
different kinds of suffering. When it comes to the mystery and ministry of human pain and anguish, Job is
the book we turn to for enlightenment and comfort.
Throughout its appealing pages is the ever-present and
pressing question, Why do the innocent and the righteous suffer? Through bitter experiences Job came to
learn that "whom the Lord loves He chastens,/And
scourges every son whom He receives" (Heb. 12:6).
The sufferings that Job endured, ones that were inflicted by Satan yet permitted and prescribed by God,

were of a varied nature. *Materially,* he suffered the loss of all the increase of his substance. Oxen, asses, sheep, and camels were both confiscated and slain, and a great wind destroyed the house of his eldest son. Job's servants, who cared for his land and cattle, were slain. *Physically,* Job was smitten with terrible suffering, for Satan inflicted sore boils upon the whole of his body. Misery, sighing, roarings, and fear were all his. Job spoke of his flesh being "caked with worms and dust,/ My skin is cracked," polluting even his garments (7:5; 30:18). *Emotionally,* he met with suffering when his wife failed to console him in his grief and told him to curse God and die. His so-called friends failed to strengthen his weak hands and feeble knees. They proved themselves to be poor comforters.

Then there were the satanic attacks, designed to weaken Job's faith and confidence in God. Satan challenged God to rob Job of all he had and cripple his body with pain and disease. Then, Satan declared, Job would curse God to His face. In a touching appeal to his friend, Eliphaz, Job said, "The arrows of the Almighty are within me;/My spirit drinks in their poison" (6:4). His friends came to "scorn" him (16:20) and to declare that his material and physical sufferings were the "portion from God for a wicked man" (20:29). But he drank up all "scorn like water" (34:7).

As he endured the scourge of Satan and the scorn of friends, Job let his "eyes pour out tears to God" (16:20). Amid his suffering, he did not complain or lose his confidence in God; hence, his challenge to all assailing him, "Though He slay me, yet will I trust Him" (13:15). His became the hope that his loathsome "flesh shall be young like a child's" and that he would return to the bloom "of his youth" (33:25). The trials, losses, and sufferings heaped upon Job made him long for death, but God did not slay him.

The Bible student discovers frequent references to death in the Book of Job. The patriarch's wife wished her husband to die cursing God (see 2:9). His friends, who were like powerless physicians, urged him as a hypocrite and a liar to give up the ghost (see 11:20), and even poor Job himself with nothing left worth living for asked this question:

Why then have You brought me out of the womb?
Oh, that I had perished and no eye had seen me! (10:18).

But Job lived to see a better day, and when ultimately he did die, he was an old man of over two hundred years; he had "lived one hundred and forty years" more. Indeed, he was "old and full of days" (42:16–17).

10

Its Doctrines

THEOLOGY

In earlier times theology was considered the "queen of the sciences." Originally this term was specifically applied to God, *theos* meaning "God." Thus, *theology* was the science, or study, of God. The contention of evolutionists, religious or otherwise, is that back in the distant past when Job lived, the human race was in its infancy, and that, consequently, man had a very limited, crude conception of the nature and character of God, but that with his gradual progress, a clearer revelation became his.

Without doubt, there is an evolution in the Bible regarding the purpose of God, seeing Scripture is a divine, progressive revelation, but this is a different matter. Further, the revelation of God unfolded in Job is all the more remarkable when one remembers that the Book of Job is not Jewish and that the characters referred to therein came from Gentile countries. After the millennia since Job lived, we may have a clearer vision of God than he had, seeing we look upon God in the face of His beloved Son, Jesus Christ. But no great, outstanding trait of the Divine Character has been added since Job's day. Job and other persons in the book did not deem God a mere tribal deity. They referred to these divine attributes: supreme, independent, holy, and incorruptible (22:2–4); immortal and eternal (10:5); spiritual and invisible (9:11; 26:13); Hearer and Answerer of prayer (22:27); King of Kings (34:18–19); Preserver of men (12:10; 33:28); Giver of wisdom (35:11); and Ruler of nations (12:23).

If it be true, as liberal theologians assert, that man slowly and gradually arrived at the present conception of God's being and nature, how can they explain the clear revelation of God that Job and others of his time had before the Bible as a book was in existence? Matthew Henry's accurate comment on this matter in his *Commentary on the Whole Bible* is worthy of committal to memory by every student of Scripture:

> Job is a monument of primitive theology. The first and great principles of the light of nature, on which natural religion is founded, are here, in a warm, and long, and learned dispute, not only taken for granted on all sides, and not the least doubt made of them, but by common consent plainly laid down as eternal truths, illustrated and urged as affecting commanding truths. Were ever the Being of God, His glorious attributes and perfections, His unsearchable wisdom, His irresistible power, His inconceivable glory, His inflexible justice, and His incontestable sovereignty discoursed of with more clearness, fulness, reverence, and divine eloquence, than in this Book?

The term *theology*, however, has become a more general term expressing not only truths concerning God, but also of subjects relative to Him and of man's duty toward Him. You might ask: Do we find such a compendium of theological truth in this venerable book? Yes. Review the key words already cited. Then, with the aid of a concordance, trace themes such as these: sanctification (1:5); chastisement (5:17); righteousness (8:6); resurrection (14:14; 19:25–26); prayer (16:17); justification (36:23); and omnipotence (42:2).

Although Job lived many centuries before the clearer and fuller revelation of the New Testament, he had a concept of the Trinity, composed of Three Persons in One.

An Omnipotent God—"I know that You can do everything" (42:2).

A Personal Redeemer—"I know that my Redeemer lives" (19:25).

The Life-giving Spirit—"The Spirit of God . . . gives me life" (33:4).

We must be careful not to build up any doctrine upon its aspects revealed in only one book or passage of the Bible. Such a method has been the cause of countless errors. Scripture is a divine library, made up of sixty-six books. The careful student must gather all the combined truth on any given theme in all of these, before dividing any phase of the word of truth.

HAMARTIALOGY

Hamartia is the Greek word for "sin." *Hamartialogy* is the science associated with the nature and effects of sin. The Book of Job, which if the first book to be written, has important insights about the doctrine of human depravity (see 15:14–16). Grouping together the passages related to sin, we can discover a great deal about its forms and its dread consequences, both here and hereafter. The deep, moral root in Job's heart was that of self-righteousness which had to be brought to the surface, judged, and removed. Job was a real child of God. Yet somehow he had never measured himself against the divine standard nor sounded the depth of his own nature.

Twice over we are told that in spite of his extreme sufferings, Job sinned not with his lips. Facing the mystery of God's permissive will in all that he endured, he never "charge[d] God with wrong" (1:22; see 2:10). As his tribulation continued, Job came to confess his sin (see 10:14–15). Others had sinned against him and faced divine judgment (see 8:4, 20). Anticipating the Pauline axiom that we reap what we sow, Eliphaz declared that they who "sow trouble reap the same" (4:8). Although in triumph Job could confess, "Though He slay me, yet will I trust Him"(13:15), he did not shrink from a divine exposure of his "iniquities," "transgression," and "sin" (13:23). Before his speeches were ended, he called upon the Almighty to reveal any hidden "iniquity in my bosom" (31:33). Elihu assured Job that if he had sinned, God was able to deliver his soul from going "down to the Pit" (33:27–28), on the basis of the forsaking of all revealed "iniquity" (34:32). Standing in the white light of divine holiness, Job cried, "Behold, I am vile" (40:4) and "I abhor myself,/And repent in dust and ashes" (42:6).

SOTERIOLOGY

The term *science* means not only any branch of knowledge, but also systematic and formulated knowledge. For instance, *soterios* is the Greek for "saving," while *Soter* means "Savior." But while Job mentioned the science appertaining to redemption, we cannot formulate the doctrine of salvation on his references alone. Job never had the clearer revelation of salvation that the New Testament presents. Much that is involved in the redemption of the soul was a mystery hidden from the patriarch. Yet some great passages in his book prove that he understood in some measure. He saw the need of a Redeemer able to meet the just claims of divine holiness, Who was also qualified to deliver man from sin.

The God Who "charges His angels" with folly would not pass over the guilt of mortal man (4:17–19). A human being can only be just in God's sight through the ministry of the "mediator" between God and the sinner (9:32–35). Job knew that his salvation was not *something* but *SOMEONE:* "He also shall be my salvation" (13:16). Then there is that remarkable statement in the chapter where Job confessed his sublime faith, "For I know that my Redeemer lives . . . in my flesh I shall see God" (19:25–26). Whether Job had received a divine revelation of the coming Savior, as Abraham and Moses had, we cannot say. But of this we can be certain, Job knew enough of God's salvation to warrant his faith that he would ultimately "see" God for himself (19:27).

DEMONOLOGY

We now come to the science dealing with evil spirits and their agency. *Daimon* is the Greek word for "spirit," which in later Greek came to mean a "devil." Upon the subjects of demons, as agents of the Devil, nothing is recorded in the Book of Job. Only the Prince of Demons, the archenemy of God and man, is mentioned. *Satan* is referred to some thirteen times in the first two chapters. Dr. A. T. Pierson wrote of the importance of what he called "The Law of First Mention." In Job we have the first mention of the Devil as *Satan*, the Hebrew word meaning "adversary." In this book, then, breathing the air of antiquity as it does, we can learn one or two fundamental truths of him who caused earth's first man and wife to sin.

The consistent testimony of Scripture as a whole is that Satan is the unceasing, untiring adversary of both God and man. Ages later than Job, John described Satan as "the accuser of our brethren" (Rev. 12:10). This is the same role he played when he maligned Job before God.

An aspect of satanic assaults we must not lose sight of is that which was so succinctly expressed by John Newton, "Satan can only go the length of his chain." God gave him permission to test Job's faith, but in effect said, "You may go so far, but no further." Did not James declare long centuries after Job that if Satan is resisted by those resting in Calvary's victory of him, that he "will flee" from them? (See James 4:7.) What is gained from Job's references to Satan's personality, character, activity, and hatred must be added to the fuller revelation of his diabolical activities the rest of Scripture presents. The contemporary believer should never grow lax and lazy, thinking that Satan is powerless. The Christian should be alert to his demonic wiles.

ESCHATOLOGY

Here is the science or doctrine dealing with last things, such as death, Christ's return, judgment, and the soul's state after death. The term is from *eschatos* (last). It is true that we must go to the New Testament for the full and final revelation of all aspects of eschatological truth. It is only through all that Christ accomplished that life and immortality have been "brought to light" or fully manifested. Yet the deep questions of death and the hereafter concerned the hearts of ancient people as well as our own. Passages as to the future are too numerous to mention, but here are a few that drew aside the veil and gave those in past ages much comfort and hope.

Man has only an appointed time on earth. God and man will come together in judgment (see 9:32). Once man leaves the earth, he will not return to it. For the believer, the land beyond the shadow of death is not one of darkness. Cut down as a tree, man does not cease to be. If he dies, he will live again (see 14:1–14) and, at the latter day, see God (see 19:27). Hell may be naked, and final destruction destitute of a "covering," but for the righteous, their eyes will behold the Savior (see 26:6). When Job died "old and full of days," it was with the blessed assurance that he would see his Redeemer in a tearless world and there understand the things too wonderful for him to know while in the flesh. What a joy it will be to meet Job in the presence of Him he so magnificently honored in the fires of affliction!

11

Its Dramatic Style and Characters

Bible scholars differ as to the exact style of this unique book. For instance, some simply treat it as a didactic poem or an epic while others treat it as a drama.

A Didactic Poem. Didactic means "fitted to teach, instructive." Surely no other book can touch the spiritual instruction permeating this book. It sets forth in poetical form the life of one who, for all time, will remain the outstanding example of those perplexed by the question, Why do the godly suffer?

An Epic. There are those who affirm that the story of Job develops under the form of an *epic*, that is, the record of some great event in an elevated style. Thus Frederic Godet, the renowned commentator, supported this view by saying:

> There is one dramatic book in the Bible, but only one, *The Songs of Solomon*. There are two epics—That of the human conscience in conflict with the justice of God, *The Book of Job*; That of the kingdom of Satan in conflict with the Kingdom of God, *The Book of Revelation*.

Drama. Then, other scholars treat Job as a dramatic composition, or a tragedy. Daring to disagree with Godet, I deem Job to be another dramatic book in the Bible. Both in style and structure, it bears the stamp of literary art. The fact that it is a drama does not do away with its historical nature.

DRAMA IN OUTLINE

Job has been called The Book of Discipline, but dramatic events and experiences are woven into the disciplinary treatment of God's servant, making the book the world's first gripping drama involving heaven and hell. The following is a plan of the characters and scenes:

CHARACTERS	SCENES
The Lord	Heaven
Sons of God	Uz—Home of
Satan	Job
Job	Ash of Mound
Job's Wife	Restored
Three Friends	Home
Elihu	

The interplay of the above characters in Job's dramatic experiences is outlined below:

I. PROLOGUE (1:1–5)	II. DIALOGUE (1:6–42:6)	III. EPILOGUE (42:7–17)
A. *CHARACTER*	A. *HEAVENLY DIALOGUE (1:6–2:10)*	A. *VINDICATION*
	Heavenly Council (1:6–12)	
	Earthly Conflict (1:13–22)	
B. *FAMILY*	*Heavenly Council (2:1–6)*	B. *INTERCESSION*
	Earthly Conflict (2:7–10)	

72

I. PROLOGUE (1:1–5)	II. DIALOGUE (1:6–42:6)	III. EPILOGUE (42:7–17)
C. WEALTH	B. EARTHLY DIALOGUE (2:11–37:24) Comfort of Friends (2:11–13) Complaint of Job (3:1–26)	C. RESTORATION
D. PRIESTHOOD	1. First Round (4–14) a) Eliphaz (4–5); Job (6–7) b) Bildad (8); Job (9–10) c) Zophar (11); Job (12–14)	
	2. Second Round (15–21) a) Eliphaz (15); Job (16–17) b) Bildad (18); Job (19) c) Zophar (20); Job (21)	
	3. Third Round (22–31) a) Eliphaz (22); Job (23–24) b) Bildad (25); Job (26–31).	
	4. Fourth Round (32–37) Elihu. Job. Friends. God.	

I. PROLOGUE (1:1–5)	II. DIALOGUE (1:6–42:6)	III. EPILOGUE (42:7–17)

C. *HEAVENLY AND EARTHLY DIALOGUE* (38:1–42:6)
Revelation of Jehovah (38:1–40:2)
Repentance of Job (40:3–5)
Revelation of Jehovah (40:6–41:34)
Repentance of Job (42:1–6)

Before watching the drama in action, study a brief sketch of the outstanding characters involved. This may help you to appreciate the specific part each one plays.

As soon as the news spread of Job's affliction, he was visited by three friends, namely, Eliphaz the Temanite, Bildad the Shuhite, and Zophar the Naamathite. These were not mythical persons, as the facts recorded of them prove.

These three would-be comforters represent three different forces ever-prominent in seeking to solve the mysterious problem of divine government and discipline in the affairs of men. *Eliphaz* is the symbol of human experience or history. *Bildad* is the symbol of tradition or philosophy. *Zophar* is the symbol of human merit or moral law. Another character, not grouped with the three but who was the youngest of those addressing Job, was *Elihu*, the symbol of human mediation.

The three friends had one general proposition to bring before Job, namely, that all suffering is judgment

74

upon sin and that from such a thesis they would not depart until told by God that they were wrong. In their approach to Job, therefore, they contended in different ways that God is righteous. God, they claimed, prospers the just but punishes the wicked, among whom they placed Job.

Eliphaz and Bildad each addressed Job three times, Zophar twice, and Elihu once.

Eliphaz, calm, dignified, and temperate, was the eldest. He commenced the dialogue using beautiful and superb language as he enunciated the above-mentioned proposition to Job.

Bildad, the more heated, direct, and personal in his attacks upon Job, illustrated his share in the discussion in very descriptive language.

Zophar appeared to speak in a daring, hasty, impulsive mood as he distinctly held Job responsible for all the trouble that had overtaken him.

Elihu, the youngest of the group confronting Job, spoke only when all the others were silent. In his long speech, Elihu both vindicated God and reproved Job and his three friends.

It may assist us in our desire to understand this unique Book of Job if we examine more particularly the character and contentions of each of the four who took it upon themselves to show why Job suffered as he did.

1. *Eliphaz.* This descendant of Esau (see Gen. 36:4) came from Teman, which was noted for its wisdom. The name *Eliphaz* means "refined gold" or "God of fine gold" and is descriptive of the bearer, who was a law unto himself. His fine gold was the self-glory from which he would not depart. Although wise, he gloried in his wisdom and represented the orthodox wisdom of his day. As a wise man from the East, he declared that God is just and does not dispense happiness or misery in a

despotic fashion, committing to people just what He thought best. His three speeches to Job were delivered with much sacerdotal pathos.

Eliphaz was a religious dogmatist, basing all his deductions upon one remarkable experience he had had of a spirit passing before his face, thus causing his hair to stand up (see 4:12–16). From the spirit he was supposed to have received a message regarding the justice of God. Because of this solitary, unusual experience, Eliphaz became rigidly dogmatic, hard, and cruel in his demand to Job to listen to his speech. His mistake was that of trying to force Job into his mold. We must beware of following another man's experience, or even of imposing our experience upon someone else. God deals in different ways with different people, and, therefore, because no other person has traveled the road we have, we must not dogmatize as Eliphaz did about God's personal dealings. God carries out His gracious work as He deems best. We must remember that our experience may not necessarily explain, or coincide with, the mystifying experience of another.

2. *Bildad*. As a Shuhite, Bildad was a descendant of Abraham. (Shuah was a son of Abraham by Keturah, whose children were sent East [see Gen. 25:2–6].) His name possibly means "Lord of Hadad," the name *Hadad* implying "to shout." Studying the three speeches of this second figure in the drama, we can see that he was "like name, like nature," for he was inclined to be loud, insistent, and boisterous in his declarations. This Shuhite in a vehement fashion implied in the discussion opened by Eliphaz that all the extraordinary ill-fortunes of Job were certain proof of hidden and exceptional crimes of which the sufferer must have been guilty.

Although his speeches are rich in ideas, Bildad was yet a religious dogmatist whose dogmatism rested upon tradition. With proverbial wisdom and pious phrases, which abound throughout his discourses, he sought to illustrate the contention that Job was suffering because of his sin. Thus, with philosophy, wisdom, and tradition, he had searched the fathers in order to convince Job of his wrongs (see 8:8). But the wisdom of man failed to unravel the mystery of Job's anguish. From Bildad we learn not to depend on human wisdom or tradition, and never to believe something because of the mere fact that it has been handed down and accepted by each successive generation. Every man must be fully persuaded in his own mind. Above all, it is essential to realize that mere human tradition is not sufficient to explain the mysterious dealings of God Who is His own interpreter and makes things plain in His own way and time.

3. *Zophar.* He hailed from Naamah, a name signifying a "pleasant abode" (a trace of which can be found in Josh. 15:41). Zophar's name is likewise suggestive of his manner and attitude, for it means "chirping" and comes from a root word implying "to twitter." This third friend, in his two speeches to Job, dealt with profound things in a somewhat more light-hearted and flippant way than his two companions. Zophar was also a religious dogmatist, but his dogmatism rested upon what he thought he knew. He symbolized human merit or moral law and resorted to vigorous legal and religious methods. He added his quota to the problem confronting Job in a more daring way, encouraged doubtless by the previous speakers who had prepared his method of approach.

In effect, Zophar advocated good living, for if Job turned from his sin and sincerely repented, God would pardon and restore. Thus with forcible language he declared that suffering is judgment and warned the sinner to repent and thereby escape heavier punishment. But how dare any man presume to know all about God (see 11:6) and plead the worth of human merit in His sight! Scofield's comment at this verse was, "Zophar is a religious dogmatist who assumes to know all about God; what God will do in any given case, why He will do it, and all His thoughts about it. Of all forms of dogmatism this is most irreverent, and least open to reason." No flesh can glory in His presence. "Prepare your heart" (11:13) Zophar commanded Job in seeking to apply the problem on hand to Job. But preparations man cannot make; his best resolves he only breaks. No man can satisfy God by self-effort or attain to a life of righteousness that will please Him. If one has sinned and is suffering as the result of his sin, he can only be saved and delivered from its thralldom as he casts himself utterly and absolutely upon the grace of God.

4. *Elihu.* This fourth speaker, who addressed Job at length, is not named as a friend of the patriarch; yet fuller details are given of him than of the other three. Elihu was "the son of Barachel the Buzite, of the family of Ram" (32:2). Buz was the brother of Uz and the son of Nahor (see Gen. 22:20–21). Jeremiah mentioned Buz along with Teman; therefore, Buz is to be reckoned as belonging to Arab tribes (see Jer. 25:23–24). The name *Elihu* signifies, "God is Lord" or "My God is He," and in a most conspicuous fashion he set out in his dialogue to exalt the Almighty One.

This youthful, unpretentious orator reached a high level in his declaration of truth and manifested a far more just and clear spiritual conception in dealing with Job's problem than the previous three men. Yet he presented only half the truth and his appeal, although lofty and eloquent, was marred by self-assertiveness. Notice his arrogance clearly manifested in statements like these: "Great men are not always wise,/Nor do the aged always understand justice" (32:9), or "My words come from my upright heart" (33:3). An impressive question is asked, "Who is *this* who darkens counsel/By words without knowledge?" (38:2, italics added). Evidently this was Jehovah's word to Elihu, seeing Job did not reply to him as he did to the other three speakers. God laid at the feet of Elihu the fault he had sought to bring against His servant Job: "Job speaks without knowledge,/His words are without wisdom" (34:35). "Therefore Job opens his mouth in vain;/He multiplies words without knowledge" (35:16).

DRAMA IN ACTION

With its 42 characters and 1070 verses, the Book of Job is one of the most dramatic compositions ever written. Before watching the unfolding of the scenes and actors, you need to have a concrete idea as to the chief theme of the drama. The book itself has been described as a *theodicy*, from the Greek words *theos* (God) and *dikē* (justice). A theodicy is therefore a presentation of the justification of Divine Government. This theodicy is a reconciliation between the justice of God and the suffering of the righteous. While there is a definite connection between sin and suffering, the mystery of this ancient book is that of the suffering of the innocent.

The New Testament counterpart of Job is the record of the man who was born blind. The disciples, like Job's three friends, seemed to connect suffering with sin (see John 9:2). But Jesus said, "Neither this man nor his parents sinned, but that the works of God should be revealed in him" (John 9:3).

Whatever purpose God may have had in allowing the

righteous to suffer, it is evident from the experience of Job that He overrules all satanic designs and uses suffering to sanctify saints and to lead them into a deeper appreciation of His august holiness. The trials He permits in the lives of His own may appear mysterious and undeserved, but faith rests in Jesus' own assuring word: "What I am doing you do not understand now, but you will know after this" (John 13:7).

12

Its Dramatic Plot

I. PROLOGUE (1:1-5)

The first five verses of the opening scene present a glowing description of the chief actor's character, both in its Godward and manward aspects. These verses also contain a detailed account of Job's family life and associations, of his wealth, of the high esteem in which he was held, and of the spiritual influence he exerted over others. What a wonderful reputation he had! "This man was the greatest of all the people of the East" (1:3). It was most fitting on the part of Moses, if he wrote the Prologue and Epilogue of Job as some conservative scholars suggest, to give us such a wonderful introduction and ending of Job's career. These two sections throw into contrast the chastisement endured and the glory that followed. For Job there was a blessed "nevertheless afterward."

II. DIALOGUE (1:6-42:6)

A. Heavenly Dialogue (1:6-2:10)

Heavenly Council (1:6-12) The scene herewith enacted in the presence of God, if rightly understood, provides a solution to the book. Regarding some of the New Testament parables, preachers of an earlier time used to say that their key could be found hanging at the front door. The key to Job hangs at the front door. The cruel assertion of Satan regarding Job's sincerity is aimed at God's honor, seeing that both Jehovah and Job are brought to the bar by this fiendish actor in the drama. The justice of Jehovah and the virtue of Job are alike at stake and so the trials of Job are to demonstrate the utter falsity of Satan's contention.

Moreover, it is essential to remember that what passed behind the veil was hidden from Job until the end of his sufferings. This champion of God had to persevere, not by sight, but by faith. He had to endure by moral conviction that God knew best, and not by the help from the light of reason, such as his friends sought to give him. Job had to battle through the darkness to victory without the apparent help or light of God. To Job, the heavens seemed as brass, but at the curtain's descent at the end, faith was victorious and brought reward. Patience did her perfect work, and Job illustrated the New Testament assertion, "This is the victory that has overcome the world—our faith" (1 John 5:4).

Earthly Conflict (1:13–22) In these ten graphic verses, we see how Satan was permitted by God to test Job. Swiftly and mercilessly, these disasters struck: the Sabeans; then the fire of God; then the Chaldeans; and then a terrific gale. Destroyed were all of Job's livestock, servants, and, it would seem, his sons. Dramatically, the prince became a pauper. Job was stripped of material possessions, of his glory, and of his crown as the greatest man of the East. But with remarkable submission, he bowed to the will of God, recognizing in all his calamities, not the hand of the satanic accuser responsible for them, but the good hand of God. Job knew that every joy or trial came from above. At the opening stage of the conflict Job won a magnificent victory. Think of his utter destitution and desolation! Yet no moan left his lips. Sitting amid the ashes of his ruined home and thinking of all he had lost, he could yet say, "Blessed be the name of the LORD" (1:21). Could we, I wonder, endure such a catastrophe and yet not charge God foolishly or sin with our lips?

Heavenly Council (2:1–6) After his diabolical work, Satan returned to God with an account of what had transpired, and one can detect that the archenemy in the plot was conscious of partial defeat. The silent submission of Job had, at the outset, destroyed Satan's cruel accusation and slander regarding his character, for he continued to cling to God, even when there were no hedges around him. Satan, however, wanted further permission to test Job, by touching him in a more tender fashion, and God allowed the enemy to deal with His servant's body this time. In all the dealings of God it is necessary to distinguish between His *permissive* will and His *direct* will. There is also the further question in this section of the physical suffering Satan can cause.

Earthly Conflict (2:7–10) Job was thrown into the furnace of affliction, heated seven times. This time his body was attacked by a loathsome disease, said to be a form of elephantiasis. What a pitiable sight he presented as he sat on the ash-mound smitten with such a horrible malady. Think of his accumulating trials! All was gone—money, possessions, home, family, honor, and finally his health. The last arrow from Satan's quiver was yet to be shot, and it came via Job's wife as with pleading voice she entreated her husband to renounce God. Surely this must have torn Job's heart with pain. What method there was in Satan's approach! May we never be ignorant of his devices! This tempter, who succeeded in bringing about the fall of the first man through his wife, determined as a last resort to use the same weapon for the same purpose. But Job succeeded where Adam fell.

Satan's hellish accusation was that as the result of further trial and suffering Job would curse God to His face. Although he did curse the day he was born, he did not curse God. Although ignorant of Satan's slander, Job won through. During his trials, as well as throughout the debates with his friends, Job never, in any way, renounced God. As Job sat among the ashes, triumph, not defeat, was his. Behind a frowning Providence, he saw a smiling Face. Clinging to the skirt of God, Job was magnificent in the loss of all: "Shall we indeed accept good from God, and shall we not accept adversity?" (2:10). From deep, bitter experiences, Job triumphed:

> The clouds may veil the sun, and tears mine eyes,
> Still reigns my Lord beyond these curtained skies.

B. Earthly Dialogue (2:11–37:24)

Comfort of Friends (2:11–13) In these remaining verses of the second chapter we are given an account of the three friends of Job who came from their respective homes to comfort their sorrowing friend. While it is true that Job endured a good deal of personal misrepresentation from these *miserable* comforters, as he called them, it is significant that they came to Job to sympathize with him by definite appointment. The reality of their sympathy is seen in that they were willing to sit in Job's presence in unbroken silence for seven days and nights.

Complaint of Job (3:1–26) In this chapter Job broke the prolonged silence by recounting to his friends his loss, misery, and despair. Human nature is ever ready to unbosom its secrets in the presence of true friendship. There is no doubt that Job's outburst was prompted by the attitude of the three who had come to console him. It would seem as if Job's lamentation was of a threefold nature, suggested Dr. Campbell Morgan, "He lamented his Existence, his Preservation, his Continued Being." What he had greatly feared had come upon him, and he was mystified over God's action in hedging him in so that he could not escape his sufferings.

1. First Round (chapters 4–14)

SPEECHES	REPLIES
a) Eliphaz (4–5)	**Job (6–7)**
This first speaker began by bringing before Job the cause of all affliction, namely, sin. Approaching him in a very courteous, yet cold manner, Eliphaz sought to prove that all calamity is judgment upon sin. The crux of his argument was this: "Remember now, who ever perished being innocent?/Or where were the upright ever cut off?" (4:7).	The patriarch stoutly protested against the principles enunciated, and in a most graphic way he proved that calamity is the portion of both the righteous and the sinful. Protesting his innocence, Job asked, "Is there injustice on my tongue?" (6:30). Unsinning lips were his, yet he suffered.
b) Bildad (8)	**Job (9–10)**
More forceful than the previous speaker, Bildad sought to illustrate the doctrines introduced. After using natural illustrations as those referred to in 8:11–12, Bildad sum-	In a most honest fashion, Job answered Bildad. Job admitted the contention of Bildad in 8:20 with a reply in 9:2. Then he showed his own helplessness as a short-lived

marized his speech by declaring, "God will not cast away the blameless,/Nor will He uphold the evildoers" (8:20). The implication was that Job was not a perfect man, but an evildoer.

man to bring his cause before God (see 9:25). No one can understand his impoverished condition (see 9:23), but Job was content to wait for One Who would vindicate him beyond death.

c) Zophar (11)

Gathering boldness, this third friend approached Job with greater bluntness and direction than the two previous speakers who had opened up the way. Zophar advanced the personal aspect of the projected theme and applied it particularly to Job, who had sinned, but had a sinner's hope in repentance toward God: "Prepare your heart . . . stretch out your hands toward Him" (11:13).

Job (12-14)

Job's reply to Zophar was a remarkable utterance in which sarcasm abounded against all three of his so-called friends, or "forgers of lies" and "worthless physicians" as he named them (13:4). What a sarcastic touch there was in Job's taunt, "No doubt you are the people" (12:2). Job appealed to God against Zophar's interpretation of his great affliction, and in sublime language, which has brought victory to suffering saints down the ages, declared he would still "trust Him" even if slain by God (13:15). Yet honesty was his; for if his suffering was the result of sin, then he desired God to reveal the sin (see 13:22).

2. Second Round (chapters 15–21)

SPEECHES

a) Eliphaz (15)

REPLIES

Job (16–17)

Eliphaz commenced his second dialogue as one who had evidently been wounded by Job's sarcastic remarks (see 15:2), and then proceeded to maintain his original argument that Job suffered because of personal sin.

The reply of Job came from a soul feeling its agony (see 16:16). What a difference it would have made if only his friends were not "miserable comforters" (16:2–4). Yet he maintained his innocence and longed for someone rightly to understand his position (see 16:17–21).

b) Bildad (18)

Job (19)

Returning to his former method, Bildad in a brief, pointed, yet graphic address described the punishment falling upon men who, like Job, were "wicked" (18:5). Certainly his utterance was right, but its application to Job was wrong.

In his reply to Bildad, Job again described his utter destitution (see 19:9), and then affirmed his "Redeemer lives" and vindication will be his beyond death (19:25–26). Comparing his light affliction with the glory yet to be revealed, Job echoed forth the certainty of faith, that the future would clear him of all cruel accusations.

c) Zophar (20)

Job (21)

This Naamathite hastened to speak a second time because Job's last word had caused "turmoil" within him (20:2). With added force he maintained his premise that Job's suffering was the result of his sin, which now takes the form of hypocrisy (see 20:5), which cannot escape

Job boldly answered this last speech of Zophar's, as well as the whole argument advanced by all three speakers. In a clear, emphatic fashion he proved that many wicked do not suffer (see 21:7–9). He then poured contempt upon his professed friends (see 21:34), having althe judgment hypocrites deserve and receive (see 20:29).

ready taunted them to "keep mocking" once he had finished speaking (see 21:2–3).

3. Third Round (chapters 22–31)

In this next scene the dramatic feature becomes more intense. The argument advanced by the three friends that suffering springs from sin is brought to a climax. Zophar, the chirping, twittering friend, became tired of arguing and vanished from the stage. But Job rose to corresponding climaxes in protesting his innocence regarding the principle advanced, illustrated, and applied to him by his friends.

SPEECHES	REPLIES
a) Eliphaz (22)	**Job (23–24)**
In this last speech, Eliphaz charged Job with sin "without end" (22:5) and proclaimed the only hope of his restoration to divine favor (see 22:21).	In his reply, Job described his anguish (see 23:2) and expressed his yearning for a true friend (see 23:3). He then expressed his perplexity over God's noninterference in the matters of the larger world (see 24:12). He believed that God is cognizant of all things (see 24:22).
b) Bildad (25)	**Job (26–31)**
In his last speech, this Shuhite reached the climax of his argument by declaring in an eloquent way the sov-	The answer to Bildad has earned the admiration of some of the greatest minds, because of its wonderful, po-

ereignty of God (see 25:2) and His holiness. These attributes excluded Job as a suffering sinner from the Divine Presence. etic charm and beauty. Here, Job reached the climax of his defense, then described the awe-inspiring greatness of God in Creation (see ch. 26), and concluded with a stout declaration of his innocence (see 27:4–5).

There are about one hundred references to self in chapters 29 and 30, which we can call the big *I* chapters. When you come to the prominence of self, are you weighed in the balance and found wanting? We have far more light than Job had, yet alas! we are so often highminded, touchy, and easily provoked. We manifest so little of the true spirit of Christ. We know next to nothing about the knife that cut deep into Job's soul and body, but how through such misunderstanding Job persevered.

Chapter 29 presents a pathetic lament over the faded light of other days. How it reveals the deep root of self-complacency! Job had need to be stripped bare and see himself in the searching light of Divine Presence. Yet in this remarkable chapter, we look in vain for any breathings of a broken and contrite spirit. There was no self-loathing. Job referred to himself over forty times but to God only five times. (It is profitable to compare the predominance of *I* in Romans 7 to this chapter of Job.)

The egotism of chapter 29 and the bitterness of chapter 30 had to be dealt with severely, for sighs of lost greatness and bitter invectives against others do not do much good. There must come the stripping, painful process. Only out of "a broken heart" and "a contrite spirit" can God fashion character (Ps. 34:18). If we stand up for our rights and contend for our own wishes, God will not leave us in our self-confidence. Only by tearing up the roots of our self-centeredness can we give God a central place. From Job's time to the present, this has been true.

It was so with Peter whom Christ allowed to be tested by the Devil. The Apostle had to pass through the most severe and painful process in order to destroy the root of self-sufficiency. How thoroughly Peter was sifted. But when he was subdued and mellowed, the Divine Glory shone forth from Peter with a bright luster.

4. Fourth Round (chapters 32–37)

Elihu. With the entrance of this young spokesman, who must have been an earwitness to all previous dialogues, we have a new voice, speaking from a higher plane than the three friends. Elihu did not argue from the standpoint of experience, neither did he appeal to tradition as Bildad had done. Like Zophar, Elihu's accent was on legality, and thus on bringing God and the soul together. When he had finished his argument, he confessed there was no answer. God alone has the answer.

There is no question about the peculiar power of Elihu's ministry as it broke upon the troubled soul of Job. His unique dialogue stands out in vivid contrast to the one-sided, defective reasoning of the three friends. Job's lament about the need of an advocate seems to have been met in Elihu. He declared that he was Job's "spokesman before God" (33:6). Claiming inspiration for his presence and message, he expressed his eagerness to speak to Job, which eagerness was hitherto bottled up because of his youth and modesty. The words of 32:2,3 give a summary of what he had to say. In short, Elihu's contention was that calamity in the shape of trial is inflicted on the best of men, but God allows a favorable turn to take place as soon as its object has been realized. Elihu understood the difficulty of both sides. Job justified himself instead of justifying God. The three friends condemned Job instead of consoling him.

All the time we justify ourselves we must be strangers to the deep blessedness God has for those who see themselves utterly helpless from Divine Grace. The wrath of Elihu was kindled against Job because he persisted in justifying himself. When we try to raise our own morals, we lower God's standards, but if we cultivate a broken, yielding spirit, we are bound to abide by the divine revelation of ourselves. In his vindication, Elihu appeared to travel along three lines:

1. He first of all condemned Job for his self-justification (see 32:2; 33:8–9).

2. He then set out to modify the doctrine of the three friends by his affirmation that affliction is as much a warning of judgment to come as a present judgment (see 34:10–11).

3. He concluded by unveiling, in a way that completely overmasters the mind, the majesty and glory of God (see chaps. 35–37). Truly, there is nothing to be added to the climax Elihu reached (see 37:5).

C. Heavenly and Earthly Dialogue (38:1–42:6)

We now reach the climax of the drama. God spoke, and He in no way justified His silence or permissive will. He had one theme, namely, the justification of *Himself*. Because of all He is, He cannot act contrary to His nature. Job did not answer Elihu, but God answered for him, "Then the Lord answered Job" (38:1).

SPEECHES	*REPLIES*
1. Revelation of Jehovah (38:1–40:2)	Repentance of Job (40:3–5)
God began His defense of Job by unveiling His majesty	Such an unveiling had its desired effect, for Job real-

and might in the world around. This description of His creative power has never been equaled in literature. Great writers bow in reverence before such a revelation.

ized through such a revelation what he had been unconscious of before, namely, hidden sin (see 40:4). Certainly he had been outwardly religious, living to prove the Devil's lie, but his sufferings were overruled by God to show him a deeper need of Divine Grace.

2. Revelation of Jehovah (40:6–41:34)

Again the Almighty spoke, and how graciously He encouraged His servant. Then followed another wonderful panorama of God's power as the Creator that cannot be excelled, including the "behemoth" and "leviathan" passages (40:15–41:34).

Repentance of Job (42:1–6)

Completely broken down in a sublime, grand submission before God's omnipotence (see 42:2), Job passed from an attitude that had been self-centered to a God-centered one. The distance between his state at the beginning and his utter emptiness of heart at the end reveals a marked spiritual progress (compare 1:1 with 42:5–6). Had Job known Matheson's great hymn, "O Love That Wilt Not Let Me Go," he would have loved it and regarded it as a perfect commentary upon his trials and sufferings.

III. EPILOGUE (42:7–17)

Vindication. In vindicating Job, God declared that his friends had misjudged both Himself and His servant.

God did not explain the mystery of suffering but affirmed that He deserved human confidence and praise. In contrast to Elihu's contention, God showed that He could be just and yet allow the righteous to be afflicted. He may be just, apart from any suffering any man may have or not have, because He is *God*.

Intercession. What a sacred touch there is in Job's intercession for his friends (see 42:8–9). With true magnanimity, these three friends had come to comfort Job, but they were misguided in their consolations. They repented of their mistake both to God and Job and made Job the recipient of a liberal offering.

Restoration. How God-like are these words: "The LORD gave Job twice as much as he had before" (42:10). How like Him this is! We must be careful to note, however, that the idea was not "rewarded" but "blessed." Restoration did not rest upon any servile motive or works of merit. Such would have illustrated Satan's accusation that Job was good because it paid him to be. The only man God can trust with possessions, such as Job had at his latter end, is the man who like Job can trust God when all earthly treasures take wings and fly away. Thus God set His seal to the victory of Job by raising him to a greater position than he had had before. This epilogue, therefore, is a fitting close to this dramatic book. It proclaims the manifestation of a Divine Love surrounding God's own children, even though they cannot comprehend at the time the meaning of their tears.

13

Its Abiding Lessons

The lessons taught by the ancient and unique Book of Job are numerous. They cover almost every realm of life. The following list can be added to those I have mentioned in the preceding chapters.

The Insecurity of Possessions (see 1:21). In his condemnation of Job, Eliphaz accused him of stripping "the naked of their clothing" (22:6), which is not in harmony with God's evaluation of Job as a man who was perfect and upright. It is evident, however, that Job himself was "stripped" bare of all he possessed and gloried in (19:9). Yet, left naked of all his belongings, he worshiped with all humility and could triumphantly say, "The LORD gave, and the LORD has taken away;/Blessed be the name of the LORD" (1:21). Does not such a tragic loss as Job endured in a brief moment teach us to "sit loose" to things of earth? Whatever we may be stripped of, no one and nothing can ever take from us our greatest Treasure, our Savior and Friend.

The Brevity of Life (see 7:6). The preacher will find the Book of Job rich in its similes on the brevity of life: "My days are swifter than a weaver's shuttle" (7:6); "My life is a breath" (7:7); "My days are swifter than a runner" (9:25); and "They pass by like swift ships,/Like an eagle swooping on its prey" (9:26). These, and other expressive figures of speech Job used, remind us that "life is very brief, like the falling of a leaf," and that it is necessary to be ready to meet God when worms commence to destroy the body.

The Importance of Speech (see 6:5). James reminded us that a Christian with a controlled tongue is able "to bridle the whole body" (3:1–12). How different the speeches of the three friends would have been, as they poured out words, words, words, if only they had had the practical advice of James before them. From the thirty-eight references to *words* in the Book of Job, we learn when and when not to speak, as well as how to speak. The basic text in this book made up of divine, satanic, and human speeches is

Teach me, and I will hold my tongue. . . .
How forceful are right words!
But what does your arguing prove? (Job 6:24–25).

May yours ever be the conversation that exalts the Gospel of Christ!

The Source of Uncharitableness (see 1:9–12). A litany in the Anglican *Book of Common Prayer* speaks of "The crafts and assaults of the Devil—envy, hatred, and malice, and all uncharitableness." These words are in agreement with the portion we are considering here. The Devil is certainly unmasked as the source of all severity of judgment of others. What wrong motives did this fiendish adversary attribute to Job? Do we not often sin against others by accusing them of wrong motives? A character can be damaged by false and malignant gossip. How hellish it was of Satan to suggest to God that Job served Him simply because of the prosperity He had endowed him with. The slanderous statement recoiled on Satan, for when Job was stripped bare and suffered bodily affliction, he could still say, "Though He slay me, yet will I trust Him" (13:15). This proved that he served God for nought, for no material reward. Augustus Hare in *The Story of My Life* quoted these lines:

> If your lips would keep from slips
> Of five things have a care:
> To whom you speak, of whom you speak,
> And how, and when, and where.

May care be yours when giving an assessment, always remembering the verse attributed to various authors:

> And so much bad in the best of us,
> That it hardly becomes any of us
> To talk about the rest of us.

The Virtue of Humility (see 32:4–8). What wealth of material there is in the humble attitude of the youthful Elihu for us who seek to instruct youth in the observance of good manners. This son of Barachel knew his place, and, as the youngest to address Job, he never spoke until his elders, including Job, had spoken. They were both "gray-haired" and "aged" (15:10), but Elihu was young in comparison. In all deference then to old age, he said, "I was afraid,/And dared not declare my opinion to you" (32:6). He certainly knew how to keep his place and did not speak to Job until he was inspired to do so by the Holy Spirit. When Elihu opened his young lips, he was full of matter, seeing the Spirit within him compelled him to speak (see 32:8,18).

The Need of Divine Instruction (see 34:32). The close reader will have noticed that the Book of Job has a great deal to say about the term *teach*. If the areas of instruction where the word is used are studied, one soon realizes how much there is to learn—and unlearn. Surely no more pointed prayer could leave our lips as a daily petition as we come to the Scriptures or face the perplexities of life than the one Elihu offered:

Teach me what I do not see;
If I have done iniquity, I will do no more (34:32).

Here *revelation* results in *sanctification*. This is ever the effect of meditating upon what God reveals by His Spirit through the Word of God. "You are already clean," said Jesus, "because of the word which I have spoken to you" (John 15:3).

The Secret of Patience. Job lived the answer to the problem of his suffering and taught us by his personal example. Across the pages of Job we can inscribe the declaration of Paul, "Now we see in a mirror, dimly, but then face to face" (1 Cor. 13:12). In His dealings with Job, God hid His smiling face behind a frowning Providence; but at the end the shadows lifted, and Job could say, "Now my eye sees You" (Job 42:5).

The greatest lesson James learned from the life and sufferings of Job was *patience*. James presented the patriarch as the model of such a virtue to all who would learn in patience to possess their souls (see James 1:2–4; 5:7,11). The trying of Job's faith surely worked patience, for he was convinced that the Judge of all the earth can do nothing but that which is right. Many anxious Christians certainly have need of patience, and God is able to meet the need in a liberal fashion.

> Blind unbelief is sure to err,
> And scan His work in vain.
> God is His own Interpreter,
> And He will make it plain.

The Value of Prayer. What a precious handbook on the benefits and blessedness of prayer Job is! As an intercessor who could pray for the friends who had misunderstood and maligned him, Job was a forerunner of Jesus Who not only prayed for His friends, but made intercession for transgressors. From the chain of passages dealing with prayer, a preacher can preach or a layperson can fashion an effective talk on such a theme: restrained prayer (15:4); pure prayer (16:17); profitable prayer (21:15); answered prayer (8:5; 22:27); acceptable prayer (33:26); and intercessory prayer (42:8,10).

The Fact of Human Depravity. If Job is the oldest book in the world, then the depravity of man goes back to the cradle of humanity. The destruction of Sodom and Gomorrah occurred in the vicinity of the country where Job resided. The hopelessness of sinful man to do anything to save himself is suggested by Job's question: "Who can bring a clean thing out of an unclean?/No one!" (14:4). Eliphaz said that "the heavens are not pure in His sight" (15:15), which is true, seeing they form the abode of Satan and the angels that fell with him (see Eph. 6:12). What ancient words could be truer of our modern society than this:

Man, who is abominable and filthy,
Who drinks iniquity like water! (15:16).

Not one of us can say, "There is no iniquity in me" (33:9). Rather we must confess, "I have sinned" (33:27). Apart from grace, our "wound is incurable" (34:6), but God is gracious and has made it possible for sinners to be saved from going into "the Pit" of hell (33:24,28). What exuberance there is in the exclamation, "I have found a ransom" (33:24).

Perhaps the most blessed message of Job is the confession, "I know that my Redeemer lives" (19:25). He Who bore our iniquity is the only One Who can bring a clean thing out of an unclean. Through His matchless grace, the most iniquitous of sinners can be fashioned into a new creature. The last words of Horace Greeley, journalist and founder of the New York *Tribune*, were, "I know that my Redeemer liveth."

Dr. F. E. Clark drew attention to the fact that as the massive hands of the great clock Big Ben mark the completion of each hour, it thunders forth in loud peal over the Houses of Parliament in London. Yet at the end of each quarter hour, the melody played upon the musical chimes consists of a few notes from Handel's magnificent oratorio, *The Messiah*. Thus, for eight miles around in the famous City of London, every fifteen minutes multitudes can hear the sweet, evangelical air, "I know that my Redeemer liveth." Palaces, slums, and hovels alike within the City receive the glad tidings. The world, with its limitless need, must hear and heed the most joyous chorus, "I know that my Redeemer liveth," if it is to be saved from further chaos and destruction.

The Nature of Self-revelation. A striking feature of Job's poignant experience is that he would not surrender his trust in God, but neither would he cease from vindicating himself. To his friends he boasted, "I am not inferior to you" (13:2). Then was it right for him to confess, "I will defend my *own ways* before Him" (13:15, italics added)? In Job's utterance, the *I* occurs about two hundred fifty times. One purpose of God in the trials He permitted His servant to endure was to change the *I* into *Thou*. The more Job knew and saw of God, the less he thought of himself.

It would seem as if he knew little of the sinfulness and deceit of the human heart even though he was widely respected as the greatest of all men in the East. God's dealing with His servant, however, brought him to realize the undiscovered depths of evil within himself and to cry, "Behold, I am vile. . . . Therefore I abhor myself,/ And repent in dust and ashes" (40:4; 42:6). In this connection, it is profitable to trace some of the *I*'s Job used during his severe trials. (Note: I have italicized the *I* in each instance.)

1. The *I* of Self-occupation and Prosperity, "Oh, that *I* were as in months past" (29:2; see also 29:4).

2. The *I* of Adversity, "When *I* looked for good, evil came to me" (30:26). (In chapters 29 and 30 alone, we have thirty-four occurrences of this personal pronoun.)

3. The *I* of Self-righteousness, "If *I* have walked with falsehood" (31:5). The personal pronoun is often used to protect his innocence.

4. The *I* of Self-revelation, "Behold, *I* am vile" (40:4).

5. The *I* of Realized Nothingness, "*I* abhor myself,/ And repent in dust and ashes" (42:6).

The Rewards of Providence. Even when Bildad in his first speech accused Job of hypocrisy, he predicted that Job would yet emerge from all his suffering greatly enriched: "Though your beginning was small,/Yet your latter end would increase abundantly" (8:7). And increase it did, for God gave Job twice as much as he had before. James bade us remember "the end intended by the Lord" in Job's endurance and patience, and how He manifested Himself as being "very compassionate and merciful" (James 5:11). He does not willingly afflict the sons of men, but has a heart of mercy. Because of His omniscience, He knows what is best for every child of His. As He is trusted, He enriches them beyond all reckoning. What was the "nevertheless afterward" for Job after patience had had her perfect work?

At the first, Job was the owner of 7,000 sheep. At the last, he had 14,000.

At the first, Job possessed 3,000 camels. At the last, 6,000 were his.

At the first, Job had 500 yoke of oxen. At the last, he had at least 1,000.

At the first, Job could count 500 female donkeys. At the last, the number was 1,000.

At the first, Job was the father of 7 sons and 3 daughters. At the last, he had—not as we would expect 14 sons and 6 daughters—but strangely the original number repeated, 7 sons and 3 daughters (see 1:2; 42:13). Job knew that his original camels, sheep, and oxen when once lost were lost forever, but he must not look on his sons and daughters as lost even though they perished when tragedy overtook his household. Job's children were also doubled, for ten waited for him in heaven and ten more were given to him as God blessed him. God doubled his family, as truly as He doubled his flocks, even though the first half of his children were in their heavenly home and the last half were given to him to live in peace in their earthly home.

The Hope of Resurrection. Although Job did not possess the clear revelation of the New Testament regarding the hope of immortality, the doctrine of the future life gleams forth like a solitary star in the darkness of his age. Job asked the question, "If a man dies, shall he live again?" (14:14), and as he anticipated the grave in which worms would destroy his diseased body, he answered his own question in a triumphant fashion when he declared, "In my flesh [his glorified body] I shall see God,/ Whom I shall see for myself" (19:26–27). Job cited an illustration of a chopped-down tree from the natural world as proof of the Resurrection (see 14:7–9). Wonderful, is it not, that the most ancient book in the world teaches the comforting doctrine of life beyond the grave?

The closing of Job as given in the Septuagint contains among other added sayings, this most suggestive one

"It is written that he will rise again with those whom the Lord raiseth."

As the curtain falls on the final act of the dramatic experiences of Job, how evident is his progress. Consider the distance between his state at the beginning, then his utter emptiness and brokenness of heart, and finally his prosperous emergence from all his trials. All Job's friends left him in the dust of humiliation, but he persevered to a new outlook on life, to new thoughts about God, and to new thoughts about himself, his friends, his circumstances, and all people. Job had to endure his mysterious sufferings without the apparent help of the light of God. Satan tried to destroy Job's faith and integrity by all he endured. But God overruled.

He would have us see, not so much Job himself, but the mystery of Providence, the malice of Satan, and the spiritual and material good in suffering. Traces of the influence of these issues are likewise produced in many of the Psalms.

Ultimately Job received the garment of praise for the spirit of heaviness. His life was laid on a loom to a pattern God saw, but Job did not. The patriarch used the illustration of a weaver's shuttle in respect to the experiences of life, going from one side—sorrow—to the other side—joy and blessedness. In the end the heavenly Weaver displays the finished garment, revealing that the dark colors were as needful to complete His perfect design as the bright colors.

Part Two

MODERN INSIGHTS
FOR MEDITATION

14

The Gains and Losses of Life

The LORD gave, and the LORD has taken away;
Blessed be the name of the LORD" (Job 1:21).

The life of all men is one of constant *receiving* and *losing*. What they have today may be gone tomorrow. *Gains* and *losses*—how they make life suspenseful for each of us. But all is well if we are resting in Him who is unchangeable—the same yesterday, today, and forever.

The Book of Job is one of the grandest sections of Divine Scripture, and Job himself one of its most compelling personalities. All that is known of his history is found in the book bearing his name. He lived in the land of Uz, was known as "the greatest of all the people of the East," and was the father of ten children (1:1–3).

Conspicuous in his life were the possessions the Lord took away from him and his reaction to the sovereignty of God. There is no evidence that his deprivations were the result of any secret and condemned sin harbored within his heart. Campbell Morgan in his *Messages of Bible Books* indicated that the Book of Job bears qualities that can be expressed by three words, namely, *sin, sorrow,* and *silence.* But while Job had sorrow and silence aplenty, there is no mention of sin as being responsible for all that befell him. In spite of all that he endured, the record states that, "In all this Job did not sin nor charge God with wrong" (1:22). All he could say was that the Lord who gave him all he had also took it away.

I ask you to consider Job as a true human being, "blameless and upright, and one who feared God and shunned evil" (1:1). Even when tempted by Satan and urged by his wife to curse the God permitting his losses, he "did not sin with his lips" (2:10) in his replies. He earned the commendation of God: "There is none like him on the earth, a blameless and upright man, one who fears God and shuns evil . . . he holds fast to his integrity" (2:3). Twice over is mentioned, along with Noah and Daniel in connection with righteousness when the state of Israel had become so iniquitous, that if these three true men had been there, their righteousness would have delivered their own souls, but not so much as one son or daughter (see Ezek. 14:20). When we come to the New Testament, Job is also held up as an example of patient endurance and of the Lord's compassion and tender mercy (see James 5:11).

Let us look for a moment at all of which Job was deprived, constraining him to say these words:

Naked I came from my mother's womb,
And naked shall I return there.
The LORD gave, and the LORD has taken away (1:21).

Job came to learn, however, how to change his agony into an anthem, and all his moaning into a song, "Blessed be the name of the LORD" (1:21).

The Loss of Wealth. In a very short time Job passed from plenitude to poverty. Material possessions were swept away. Once rich, he became poor when his property was destroyed by the raiding of the Sabeans and the Chaldeans. But his reaction to such a deprivation was, "He fell to the ground and worshiped" (1:20).

The Loss of Health. Permitted by God to test Job, Satan "struck Job with painful boils from the sole of his foot to the crown of his head." To relieve himself of great pain he took "a potsherd with which to scrape himself while he sat in midst of the ashes" (2:7–8). Yet although such physical pain and anguish were his, he "did not sin with his lips," by cursing God as urged to do by his wife. "Shall we indeed accept good from God, and shall we not accept adversity?" (2:10). What triumph over trial was Job's!

> The loss of wealth is much,
> The loss of health is more,
> The loss of soul is such a loss,
> That nothing can restore.

With all his losses, Job never lost his soul. He ever had a benediction for batterings he endured.

The Loss of Family. Destructive forces, natural and human, denuded Job still further. Both the Sabeans and the Chaldeans plundered and killed the servants and cattle of Job. A most disastrous wilderness wind destroyed the house in which his sons and daughters were feasting and killed the young men who were present. Such a terrible deprivation caused Job much grief, yet he could still worship. Although stripped naked, he could bless the name of the Lord. Submission to the sovereign will of God maintained the spiritual composure of His servant, enabling him to find an occasion for praise even in adversity. In his hour of desolation, Job was unusually sensitive to God's confronting and consoling presence.

The Loss of Love's Partnership. The sight of Job's boil-covered body and of the pain he suffered was too much for his unnamed wife, who played a role similar to that of Eve. Each woman yielded to Satan and became his tool. Thus, Job's wife assisted Satan in his war against

Job's integrity. "Curse [or renounce] God and die!" (2:9). Through the past there had existed the partnership of love and faith between Job and his wife, but now it was ended. Job was left to an awful loneliness of heart. Although most sorely tried, Job could exclaim, "Blessed be the name of the LORD," but his wife urged him to change such a benediction to a curse, "Cursed be the name of the LORD."

A striking omission comes after this episode. Defeated Satan is not mentioned again in the book, nor is Job's wife, apart from casual references (see 19:17; 31:10). Satan prophesied that Job would curse God, but he blessed Him instead. In the Hebrew there is a play on one root word for "cursing" and "blessed." Satan used the word with the meaning of "cursing," but Job employed the meaning of "blessing." *The Wycliff Bible Commentary* gives the following application of this testing that Job endured:

> The triumph of Job's patience over the Adversary's malice provided a seal, especially for the ages before the Incarnation of God's promise that He would bestow on the faithful the gift of eternal salvation through the Christ to come.

The Loss of Friends. The compelling story of Job's three friends, Eliphaz the Temanite, Bildad the Shuhite, and Zophar the Naamathite, occupies the bulk of the Book of Job (see 2:11–32:1). Learning of their friend's plight, they journeyed from afar to commiserate with him. What a shock the friends received the moment they saw Job but failed to recognize him.

They found things different from what they had expected. Though aware of Job's calamities, they were not prepared for what they saw. Their presence afforded Job little sympathy. Evidently the disease with which Satan had inflicted Job was still visible on *face* and *form* and such a wretched condition led the three friends to assume that his awful sight could mean nothing but the judgment of God upon evil in Job's heart and life. Thus far, Job had not sinned with his lips, but his three friends brought out what was in his *heart*. Though they did not understand God's sovereign government with Job, they became guilty of false accusation when they said many right things as to that government in other cases.

Thus, instead of consoling Job, the three friends sat silent and dismayed for seven days and seven nights, as if mourning for the dead (see Gen. 50:10; 1 Sam. 31:13). They hid, as it were, their faces from him; he was despised, and they esteemed him not. These prophetic words applicable to the Son of God were the reaction of Job's friends toward him. They felt the curse upon him was justified.

The character of each friend was revealed in their speeches.

Eliphaz emphasized a personal experience and was somewhat mysterious and remarkable. Although he uttered many true things, and that eloquently, he was presented as being hard, dogmatic, and cruel. He must be heard because of his unique experience. "I have seen, / Those who plow iniquity/And sow trouble reap the same" (4:8).

Bildad was the voice of tradition and the authority of antiquity. His dogmatism was somewhat superficial, being founded upon proverbial wisdom, and thus deemed pious as his discourses reveal (see 8:1–22; 18:1–21). He said that Job's platitudes were true enough, but then everyone knew them, nor did they shed any light on such a problem as Job's.

Zophar declared law and righteousness. In a dogmatic way he presumed to know all about God. Said Zophar to Job, "If iniquity were in your hand, and you put it far away, . . ./ Then surely you could lift up your face without spot" (11:14–15).

The arguments of his friends led Job to assert his integrity among men and to confess to God, "You know that I am not wicked" (10:7). What the three friends could not explain was Job's sense that it was God who was dealing with him and that he was not suffering from ordinary causes. Somehow, Job felt wounded in the house of his friends. The ultimate loss of their friendship caused Job to feel that he had lost his final human anchorage, as he described in his familiar words, "My close friends have forgotten me" (19:14).

Thus stripped of all men he had come to lean upon, what was left to Job in his nakedness? *God was left!* Job had maintained his sense of intimate relationship with Him and his recognition of His government over evil. He never denied God in spite of all his tribulation. Think of his faith in the omnipotence of God, expressed in the statement, "I know that You can do everything" (42:2).

There was the assurance that God's favor was his, evident in the symbol Job used, "His lamp shone upon my head" (29:3). Michelangelo made a special cap to which he fixed a candle for night work. In this way the light always shone clearly on the part of the statue he was working. In Job's dark days, the way was always clear before him; God was the candle that shone from his head. May He Who is the Light of the world ever illumine our paths!

When Job's sorrow was ended and his Jordan passed, what a glorious triumph was his after all his tribulation. As Job prayed for the three friends who had failed him,

God graciously restored all he had been deprived of and gave him twice as much as he had had before. All his relatives rallied round him, and God blessed his latter days more than his early days. He also found great joy in his family; he lived 140 years after the passing of all his deprivations, in harmony with his children and grandchildren for four generations, before he died full of days. Truly Job's life was a remarkable exhibition of God's grace and sovereign government!

A Type of Jesus. It is but fitting to end this meditation with a further view of Job as a type of Jesus, who was to experience the stripping away of many things. Holy, harmless, undefiled, separate from sinners while among sinners, Jesus suffered greatly as the Man of Sorrows. For some thirty years He lived in His Nazareth home in which He was not understood, for even His brothers and sisters did not believe in Him. Although Jesus was born King of the Jews, they failed to recognize His sovereignty. He came to His own, and His own did not receive Him but finally crucified Him. During His brief ministry, many deprivations were His. He had no certain dwelling place—nowhere to lay His head. Dependence on others for water and meat must have been hard for Jesus to endure, seeing He was able miraculously to provide food for thousands of hungry people. But He never performed a miracle to relieve any physical or material need of His own. When He came to die, the soldiers literally stripped Him. They shared His garments among them, leaving Him to die in nakedness and shame. On the cross He was momentarily deprived of the assurance of His Father's presence and protection, "My God, My God, why have You forsaken Me?" (Matt. 27:46).

In the end, like Job, Jesus died. Unlike him, He did not remain dead, but by dying He conquered death. "I am He who lives, and was dead, and behold, I am alive forevermore. Amen. And I have the keys of Hades and of Death" (Rev. 1:18).

Further, when all Job's trials were over, God gave Job twice as much as he had at the beginning. It was so with our blessed Lord Who, as He died, cried with a loud triumphant voice, "It is finished!" What was finished? With all his losses in the past, Job's crown of joy came when he could be at peace in his family circle with his children and grandchildren around him in a happy fellowship. What did Jesus finish as He died? It was "to finish His work" His Father sent Him to accomplish (see John 4:34). What was the nature of His God-given task? Was it not to die for the sin of the world, and out of all saved by His redemptive blood to form a spiritual family, the church, which is His body? All who are truly saved are His "children of the promise" (Rom. 9:8). By His sufferings, death, resurrection, ascension, and the coming of the Holy Spirit, the mystic fabric, "the church of the living God," came into being and represented twice as much as Jesus had at the beginning. With every soul saved from the guilt, power, and penalty of sin, Jesus sees anew the travail of His soul and is satisfied. His church, when complete and in the heavenly place Jesus has prepared for her, will form His crown of eternal joy.

15

God's Preserves

O thou preserver of men (Job 7:20 KJV).

When jams are made, they are placed inside glass containers and sealed in order to keep them from mildew and decay. They are often called *preserves*.

In the jar of Divine Love and Security are the Lord's children—His Preserves. "The Lord will . . . preserve me for His heavenly kingdom" (2 Tim. 4:18). We are entirely dependent upon Him for preservation; we do not have the ability to preserve ourselves. Because of the constant appeal of the old nature, we are liable to fall any day. When we would do good, evil is present. Satan is ever vigilant as the destroyer of the Lord's property. The world, the flesh, and the Devil are combined to harm us in their endeavor to nullify our security. "I know that in me (that is, in my flesh) *nothing good dwells;* for to will is present with me, but how to perform what is good I do not find" (Rom. 7:18, italics added).

How deep is our need, then, of One Who is able to keep us from falling and to present us faultless before the presence of His glory with exceeding joy. How grateful we should be for a compassionate God Who can preserve and does preserve His own as they seek to live in harmony with His will and purpose! He is our Light in darkness, our Strength in weakness, our Guide in perplexity, our Deliverer in danger and conflict, and our Preserver at all times!

As the word *preserve* means "to keep and maintain in freshness" for the purpose prepared for, let us trace the various ways our loving Preserver functions. Poor Job, with his losses and crosses, trials and testings, found it hard to accept God's watchful eye over him for his good!

The Psalms are most eloquent in extolling Divine Preservation. Personal trust in God merits His care, "Preserve me, O God, for in You I put my trust" (Ps. 16:1). "Let integrity and uprightness preserve me,/For I wait for You" (Ps. 25:21). "Blessed is he who considers the poor. . . ./The LORD will preserve him" (Ps. 41:1–2).

The teaching of Christ is most emphatic, "Whoever loses his life will preserve it" (Luke 17:33). That all the saints are God's eternal preserves is emphasized by Paul's wish for the Thessalonians that their "whole spirit, soul, and body be preserved blameless at the coming of our Lord Jesus Christ. He who calls you is faithful, who also will do it" (1 Thess. 5:23–24).

If we would be well preserved, then we must be found in the way of obedience, watching, praying, and walking humbly with the heavenly Preserver Himself every moment of the day. It is folly to think ourselves safe from satanic attack unless we cultivate a communion with the Holy Spirit, Who is within us to preserve us against every foe.

Let us in life, in death,
Thy stedfast truth declare,
And publish with our latest breath
Thy love and guardian care.
—Paul Gerhardt

16

Excellencies of a Perfect Man

Behold, God will not cast away the blameless,
Nor will He uphold the evildoers.
He will yet fill your mouth with laughing. . . .
Those who hate you will be clothed with shame,
And the dwelling place of the wicked will come to
    nothing (Job 8:20–22).

In his first address to Job, Bildad mistook Job's character, a mistake common to all three friends of the patriarch. Although Bildad's approach to Job was un-merited, he yet uttered the eternal principle that moral character can determine man's destiny.

The message opens with the positive declaration that "God will not cast away the blameless" (8:20; perfect man, KJV). What are we to understand by the *blameless*, or *perfect man*? The world has only had one absolutely perfect Man, the Man Christ Jesus. He came among imperfect men, as God's ideal Man, Whom none could convict of sin.

Any human perfection, then, is the Lord's. We are only perfect *in* Christ Jesus. Doubtless Bildad had in mind a man who had all the excellencies a good man ought to possess and exhibit. So the assertion is that the man of God whose ways are perfect will never be rejected but preserved as the apple of His eye. Adversely God will never help evildoers. He leaves them alone to struggle and stumble on. The idea of the portion before us is that of the Righteous Governor of the world saving the good, but leaving the wicked to themselves until they repent and turn to Him for mercy.

Then comes a pleasant phrase, "He will yet fill your mouth with laughing/And your lips with rejoicing" (8:21). Here Bildad expressed his belief that if Job would turn to God, he would become a happy and prosperous man. "Lips with rejoicing" means "shouting for joy"—an experience all who "walk in the light as He is in the light" (1 John 1:7) constantly enjoy. Yes, the children of the Lord have the right to shout and sing!

Bildad painted a different portrait in the next sentence, namely, all that hate God "will be clothed with shame" (8:22). The wicked hate the godly, but the time comes when the wicked are confounded and their habitations are utterly destroyed. All their mansions and summer houses come to naught. Nothing but utter destruction awaits the unrighteous. The conclusion of Bildad's message, then, enforces two aspects: the prosperous condition of the good and the disastrous condition of the wicked.

Bildad regarded Job not as a perfect man, but as a sinner and a hypocrite, and assured him that if he were indeed good that God would not forsake him but ever abide with him. Such, of course, is a truth experienced by those who are deeply conscious of inner wickedness and turn to the Savior in genuine repentance.

As an unknown poet has expressed it:

> 'Tis religion that can give
> Sweetest pleasure while we live.
> 'Tis religion that must supply
> Solid comfort when we die.

After death its joy shall be
Lasting an Eternity;
By the Living God, my Friend,
Then my bliss shall never end.

17

Not One of a Thousand

Then Job answered and said:
Truly I know it is so,
But how can a man be righteous before God?
If one wished to contend with Him,
He could not answer Him one time out of a thousand.
God is wise in heart and mighty in strength.
Who has hardened himself against Him and prospered?
(Job 9:1–4).

Chapters 9 and 10 cover Job's answer to Bildad's estimation of his character. Bildad had charged Job with being a hypocrite and, on the whole, a wicked man. But while Job, in his reply, protested against the described wickedness with which his friends charged him, he never claimed absolute perfection of life. Conscious as he was of not being perfectly holy, he was likewise conscious that he was not the wicked sinner the friends made him out to be. This is why he said, "I know it is so."

Doubtless Job was concerned about a previous statement of Bildad's, "If you were pure and upright,/Surely now He would awake for you" (8:6). The inference is that Job admitted the truth that God would ultimately appear for the needy man.

No man can appear righteous in the presence of God, Who is absolutely pure and holy. Knowing that he was innocent of the unjust charges brought against him, Job realized that in the presence of absolute holiness he could not stand and he deserved condemnation. God is righteous and requires man or woman to be righteous in His sight. But of himself, man cannot provide such required righteousness which God loves. But what He demands, He provides. He demanded righteousness and provided His beloved Son to come to earth as the personification of divine righteousness.

Then Job affirmed that God's charges against man cannot be refuted. Not "one of a thousand" (9:3 KJV) is able to do so. The term *thousand* implies the largest multitude. The thought is that no sinner in the universe can offer a defense for the slightest offense against God.

Study the magnificent designations of God, characteristic of Job's penmanship.

"Wise in heart" (9:4). The manifold wisdom of God is revealed in the whole system of Nature, in the arrangements of Providence, and above all, in the revelation and redemptive work of Christ. It is because of His perfect wisdom that He knows all about us, even the inmost depths of our being. He cannot be deceived by our falsehoods.

"Mighty in strength" (9:4). This further revelation presents God as the Almighty One. The psalmist had a similar thought: "You have a mighty arm;/Strong is Your hand, and high is Your right hand" (Ps. 89:13). Such divine power is seen in Creation. This same power is the sustenance of the universe. God is the Force of all forces, the One Whose strength is absolute, independent, illimitable, undecayable, and always allied to justice and joy.

Among Christians, we find some who are "wise in heart" but not "mighty in strength." Others are "mighty in strength" but lack a heart-wisdom. But in God, there is the blissful harmony of all noble attributes—the "fulness of all in all." This is why Job concluded by emphasizing God's invulnerability, "Who has hardened himself against Him and prospered?" (9:4). The answer is, no one! As the Eternal, Omnipotent God, He cannot be harmed or injured. It is only as we love, trust, and obey Him, always seeking to fulfill His perfect designs that we may find true prosperity. The great principle Job would have us bear in mind is that man must be one with God in the arrangements of His providence and grace. Wisdom from on high is manifest in man's constant meditating on the divine will and in his seeking to follow it.

18

The Loss of Hope is Death

The eyes of the wicked will fail,
And they shall not escape,
And their hope—loss of life! (Job 11:20).

Zophar, confronting Job as a wicked person whose trials were deserved, urged him to prepare to repent. In his defense Job answered that he was in no way inferior to his critics (see 12:1–4).

True hope is a desirable expectation, being composed of the two elements *desire* and *expectation*. It is not merely desire, for we desire many things we cannot hope for. Further, it is not expectation only, for we expect many things we do not hope for, such as adversity or infirmity.

"Hope," said Byron,

Is the rainbow to the storms of life,
The evening beam that smiles the clouds away,
And tints tomorrow with prophetic day.

But Zophar, speaking of the hope of the wicked, described it as a tragic hope—loss of life. The forfeit of a dominant hope is like death in a twofold way. First of all, death is a painful event, both physical and mental. Death implies the termination of the mystic ties that bind soul with the body and the body with all there is for it in the outward universe. For these reasons, there is a recoil from death. For the wicked, the greatest agony is not the mere death of the body but the departure of the soul to a future of black despair. In the second place, the loss of a bright hope is ruinous in that death robs the body of all its enjoyments and the wicked themselves of a bright future of eternal bliss.

But for those saved by matchless grace, "the blessed hope," the glorious appearing of the Savior is like "the beauteous sun which colors all it shines upon." Said Abraham at the death of Sarah, his wife: "Give me property for a burial place among you, that I may bury my dead out of my sight" (Gen. 23:4). He did not comprehend the same hope the Christian understands today.

For the wicked what a gloomy, hideous spirit theirs must be without hope. A soul without a bright hope is a soul without love, and a loveless soul is a soul destitute of every virtue, the cage of all the noxious reptiles of vice.

Further, it is clearly evident that the loss of life, or death of the body, means the loss of all its utility. A corpse can render no service; all power is gone. It has been said, "The tongue of the orator, the pen of the author, the chisel of the sculptor, the tool of the workman, are all still and silent forever."

Would that we could see that many around us have a desire for an enduring, eternal hope—a hope that lasts as long as the body lasts. True, there are hopes like meteors in the sky of our being, lighting for a moment before they are gone. But, as the Lord's, our present hope is great and grand, our "good hope" because it has as its object "an inheritance incorruptible." It is good also because of its foundation, namely, the promises of God Who cannot lie and Who has made us the heirs of His immutable counsel.

19

A Study on Profit and Loss

Can a man be profitable to God,
Though he who is wise may be profitable to himself?
(Job 22:2).

The opposites of *profit* and *loss* are ever before us in Scripture. Calling His disciples and people generally unto Him, Jesus proclaimed the significance of profit and loss in connection with true discipleship:

Whoever desires to save his life will lose it, but whoever loses his life for My sake and the gospel's will save it. For what will it profit a man if he gains the whole world, and loses his own soul? Or what will a man give in exchange for his soul? (Mark 8:35–37).

In chapter 22 we have the answer of Eliphaz to chapter 20, which contains Zophar's sermon on the wicked. Job said that sermon was made up of "empty words" and comfortless "falsehood" (21:34). Job earlier asked, "What profit do we have if we pray to Him?" (21:15). Eliphaz continued to accuse Job of wickedness.

Note the two related questions, "Can a man be profitable to God . . .?" and "Is it any pleasure to the Almighty that you are righteous?" (22:2,3). These questions must not be misunderstood. Eliphaz appears to suppose that Job, because of service for God, had a special claim upon His favor, but he affirmed that man can confer no favor upon God or place Him under any obligation. God is independent and supreme and too great to be benefited by man.

The sentiment of the question therefore implies that a wise man may promote his own advantage, but he cannot be of advantage to God. Human wisdom impresses people but not God. The reply of Eliphaz to Job implies that God cannot be deterred from punishing the wicked by dread of losing their favor. Neither can He be induced to bless them because they have laid Him under any obligation.

It is a false claim that the Almighty has no pleasure in the righteous. Solomon declared, "When a man's ways please the LORD,/He makes even his enemies to be at peace with him" (Prov. 16:7). The meaning of the passage, then, is that God is not dependent on man for pleasure, and He cannot be deterred from dealing justly with him because of any danger of losing anything. God has pleasure in holiness and is pleased when men are righteous. But He is not reliant on their character for His own happines or brought under any obligation by their righteousness. God is all-sufficient in Himself and has no need, therefore, to be dependent on frail, erring mortals. When the church places its reliance on a human arm, God very often suddenly knocks the prop away.

In a wider sense, the profitability of man to God, as well as for himself, and the loss he suffers if he is not profitable are before us in Scripture. God Himself is a perfect Teacher Whose instructions are always profitable for heart and life (see Is. 48:17–18). By His wisdom He directs our common sense (see Eccl. 10:10). The gods men make are "profitable for nothing" (Is. 44:10 KJV).

Addressing the elders in Ephesus, Paul affirmed, "I kept back nothing that was profitable unto you" (Acts

20:20 KJV). The Apostle had a similar commendation for two who had at one time seemed unprofitable. In writing about Mark and Onesimus, he called each "profitable" (2 Tim. 4:11; Philem. 11 KJV). Paul also reckoned that godliness is more "profitable" than bodily exercise and that Scripture is "profitable" to us in several ways (1 Tim. 4:8; 2 Tim. 3:16). In his letter to Titus, Paul outlined those things "good and profitable" for pastors to observe (Titus 3:8), things that make their progress in spiritual matters "evident to all" (1 Tim. 4:15).

How deep is the need to examine ourselves in order to discover whether we are profitable to God in our life and witness! There may be things we have counted as gain but that must be treated as loss, or not spiritually profitable in any way.

20

Beware of Snares

Snares are all around you (Job 22:10).

We seldom think of the important things Scripture has to say about snares. Several terms are used to indicate the literal snares, traps, and pits by which animals are caught. Symbolically, the word is employed to indicate the snares people lay for one another.

Especially does the Bible warn of those snares Satan lays to entrap us in his power. The Holy Spirit has depicted dangers so we will take warning. The figure of the fowler waiting to snare birds gives us an insight into the cruel, treacherous character of the enemy of our souls (see Ps.91:3). If only we could tear the mask from his seemingly beautiful face as he presents himself as "the angel of light," we would discover his cruel, ugly, diabolical grin when he succeeds in deluding us. How we would then turn from him with horror!

A skillful deceiver, Satan is bent on our destruction. The baits he uses are things people like that may not always be moral evils in themselves, such as riches, honor, and power. But finally these enticements may result in the loss of soul (see 1 Tim. 3:7; Rev. 12:9).

The Deceiver knows only too well that snares, to be effectual, must be concealed. Solomon affirmed that it is vain to set a trap in the sight of any bird; in like manner, the fisherman hides his hook when fishing. The Christian, however, led by the Holy Spirit, is "not ignorant" of Satan's devices and is on the alert for them (see 2 Cor. 2:11). Let us, then, consider some of his devices. I want to point out seven snares ever in the pathway of life.

1. THE SNARE OF PRIDE

Lest being puffed up with pride he fall into the same condemnation as the devil. . . . lest he fall into reproach and the snare of the devil (1 Tim. 3:6–7).

Solomon would have us remember, "Pride goes before destruction,/And a haughty spirit before a fall" (Prov. 16:18). How true this was in the history of Satan himself. In irony the name *Lucifer* was given to the king of Babylon, because of his pride when he said that he would exalt his throne above the stars of God. Properly such a name goes back to Satan before his fall and expulsion from heaven. *Lucifer* means "Light-Bringer," a term associated with the "day star" or "morning star" (Is. 14:12). In a past eternity, Lucifer was the head of the great angelic host, in harmony with the will of God. But his avarice led him to ape God and to exalt his "throne above the stars of God" (Is. 14:13). He was thus expelled from heaven along with the angels he had duped. He became known thereafter as *Satan*, meaning "adversary" both of God and man, and also as the *Devil* (diabolus), chief of the demons or the angels who followed him in his expulsion from the presence of God. The term *Devil* means "accuser," "to throw over," "the enemy antagonist and opposer of the saints and of all good." Although, originally, God created the Devil, He never made him a *devil*. He made him an angel with freedom of choice. Lucifer's pride changed his name and character.

Pride! What a snare! There is pride of grace, of race, and of face. We become proud over our possessions, efforts, rights, and ways. Christ desires to have us like Himself—meek and lowly in heart. Satan strives to have us like himself—proud, conceited, and adverse to all that is God-like.

Peter would have us know that the only way up is down: *"Humble* yourselves under the mighty hand of God, that He may *exalt* you in due time" (1 Pet. 5:6, italics added). May we, therefore, be found clothed with humility, for "God resists the proud,/But gives grace to the humble" (1 Pet. 5:5, quoting from Prov. 3:34).

> Our highest place, is lying low,
> At our Redeemer's feet.

2. THE SNARE OF WEALTH

Those who desire to be rich fall into temptation and a snare (1 Tim. 6:9).

Paul, who certainly knew what it was to be poor for Christ's sake, warned us. The Apostle would have us remember that the love of money—not money in itself but the passion for it—is the root of all evil and disastrous as far as Christian witness is concerned.

It is not everyone God can trust with the abundance of material possessions. As glittering gold snared Ananias and his wife to their death, so earthly riches have robbed many of the riches of divine grace. The more prominent place a person gives to money and the position it may attain, the less prominence God receives. If we strike out the *l* in *Gold* we are left with *God*—the right motto of life. If He is our sovereign Lord, we have wealth none can rob us of.

While among men, the Redeemer, who had no certain dwelling place, possessed no earthly riches. While, creatively, "all silver and gold" were His, when it came to the question of paying taxes to Caesar, whose image Roman money bore, Jesus had to say, "Bring Me a penny." He had not one of His own to use. Rich, for our sakes He became poor. How apt we are to forget that the peace of God is not to be found in worldly possessions! So many true believers have fallen into the trap of the fowler. Whether ours is much or little, may grace be ours to be content with what God has provided!

3. THE SNARE OF INDIFFERENCE

That they may come to their senses and escape the snare of the devil, having been taken captive by him to do his will (2 Tim. 2:26).

The most striking illustration of indifference in the Bible is that of the ruler Gallio who, in respect to the persecution of Sosthenes and to the defense of Jewish laws and customs, "took no notice of these things" (Acts 18:12–17). Shakespeare wrote of "the indifferent children of the earth," and there are many of them! Edmund Burke, essayist of the eighteenth century, in a letter to a friend said, "Nothing is so fatal to religion as indifference, which is, at least, half infidelity." A similar thought is expressed in G. B. Shaw's play *The Devil's Disciple:* "The worst sin towards our fellow-creatures is not to hate them, but to be indifferent to them; that's the essence of inhumanity."

Drifting into a state of spiritual slumber or unconcern or a "don't care" attitude is a snare we have to guard ourselves against. In the context, Paul urged young Timothy to avoid those foolish and ignorant disputes that foster strife (2 Tim. 2:23-26). Strifes and arguments leading to estrangements among Christians are a snare of the clever fowler to guard against. Such contentions only stir up the old nature and put the new nature to sleep. We must watch for all satanic traps and ever pray for spiritual alertness and activity.

4. THE SNARE OF IDOLATRY

Gideon made it [the golden earrings] into an ephod. . . . And all Israel played the harlot with it there. It became a snare to Gideon and to his house (Judg. 8:27).

An *ephod*, part of priestly attire, fashioned of gold and cunning linen work, was conspicuous "for glory and for beauty," (Exod. 28:2,5–14). Because of its attractiveness, the people came to seek guidance from it and to make it an object of idolatry, which was the sin of Gideon. *Wycliffe Commentary* suggests:

Gideon had an idol made, wearing an ephod similar to that worn by the high priest . . . Its erection as an object of worship marked the tragic end of the career of a truly great man. Gideon and his family suffered as the result of it. We read of the death of most of Gideon's sons because of the desire of one Abimelech to be king, Judg. 9:5. This tragedy may be traced to the idolatry that resulted from the construction of Gideon's ephod. When the ephod became an idol, it was the right thing in the wrong place. Too often, we allow right things to take a wrong place.

The question also arises, what is an *idol*? It is a thing of no value—only a molten or wooden figure. Although worshiped as a god, it is not a god. Whatever a person fashions as an idol, he makes his god. Whatever occupies the throne God ought to have is an idol. One of the most subtle, effective snares of the Devil is to misplace the Lord in our heart. A friend, self-pleasure, dress, or habit can become idolatrous, a substitute god as the ruler of our life.

The dearest idol, whate'er that idol be,
Help me to tear it from its throne, and worship only Thee.

Our safety rests not in trying to live as near the line of separation but as far as possible from every semblance of the world.

Is there a thing beneath the sun
That strives with Thee my heart to share?
Ah, tear it thence, and reign alone,
The Lord of every notion there;
Then shall my heart from earth be free,
When it hath repose in Thee.
—Gerhard Tersteegen

5. THE SNARE OF COMPROMISE

You shall destroy all the peoples whom the LORD your God delivers over to you; your eye shall have no pity on them; nor shall you serve their gods, for that will be a snare to you (Deut. 7:16).

Here Moses insisted on the absolute destruction of all Israel's foes. No pity was to be shown, for if many were spared Israel would come to mix with them, serve their gods, and thus be snared. But Israel became guilty of compromise. The message for our hearts is, "Give sin no mercy." Let God utterly slay all that is devilish in life.

Brook no compromise, no secret sympathy with anything God hates. A Christian can make no progress in spiritual things if there is entanglement in some dear habit of sin—a surrender of principle for the sake of gain.

Was this not the trap Saul fell into when he failed to obey the divine call to slay all that belonged to the foes of the Lord? He met Samuel with the triumphant news, "I have performed the commandment of the LORD." But the prophet replied, "What then is this bleating of the sheep in my ears, and the lowing of the oxen which I hear?" (1 Sam. 15:13–14). Such bleating was the evidence of compromise. Saul had to learn that God had greater delight in full obedience to His voice than in sacrifices.

If we are guilty of compromise in any direction, let us here and now accept the complete escape from such a snare.

Depart! Depart! Go out from there,
Touch no unclean thing;
Go out from the midst of her,
Be clean,
You who bear the vessels of the LORD (Is. 52:11).

6. THE SNARE OF FEAR

The fear of man brings a snare,
But whoever trusts in the LORD shall be safe (Prov. 29:25).

Fear is a snare besetting the saved and unsaved alike. *It is the snare of the sinner.* Often those who realize that they should decide for Christ fail to surrender to His claims because of the fear of the taunts they may receive from home, the office, or some other sphere of contact.

It is the snare of the saint. Fear of being an out-and-out witness in following Christ through the waters of baptism and of being fully separated from the world unto Him besets many a child of God. When the disciples saw the swords and clubs their Master faced, "They *all* forsook and fled" (Mark 14:50, italics added).

May grace be ours to live in the numerous "fear nots" of the Bible. *Fear* has a two-sided meaning. It means "a troubled, agitated frame of mind"—afraid of what overtakes one. Yet when we are exhorted to "fear God," the words imply not a cringing attitude before Him, but a reverential trust and confidence in Him as the God of love and mercy. In His teaching about the right and wrong aspects of fear, Jesus said, "Do not fear those who kill the body but cannot kill the soul. But rather fear Him who is able to deliver both soul and body in hell. . . . Do not fear therefore; you are of more value than many sparrows" (Matt. 10:28–31). It was said of John Knox that "he never feared the face of men." Fearing God, we shall not fear the face of man or the activity of demons. Courage is a gift God willingly bestows.

7. THE SNARE OF WRONG COMPANIONSHIPS

They mingled with the Gentiles
And learned their works;
They served their idols,
Which became a snare to them (Ps. 106:35–36).

These words reveal the disastrous consequences occurring to Israel for mixing with the Canaanites in the land. The company we keep can be an index of character. What a snare companions have proved to be for many professing Christians! Many young believers fail to make progress because of worldly, corrupting companionships. The desire to please carnal-minded friends is a snare to avoid. If a companion whispers in the ear, "Come along with me, there is no harm in it," resistance should be immediate and definite.

If Christians value their own souls and truly love the Savior, their *no* must be emphatic. It may mean losing a friend of the world, who is an enemy of God. We read that Peter and John, when released by the scribes and priests, "being let go, they went to their own companions" (Acts 4:23), to those true to the Lord. Theirs was a tie binding their hearts as one, a kindred fellowship like that above.

Sinners also fall into Satan's trap when they prefer the friendship and company of other sinners rather than the company of God and of those who love and serve Him. Snares, then, are round about sinners as well as saints. We must remember two important points:

1. We have a wily, cunning foe, a hellish fowler always on the lookout to entangle us in the meshes of his snares.

2. We have a wise Keeper, well able to prevent our being snared by the Devil, "Surely He shall deliver you from the snare of the fowler" (Ps. 91:3). Being omniscient, God knows all about the wiles of the Devil and is ever at hand to give us invisible protection from invisible and visible dangers. He will give us wisdom to detect and meet the cunning of the fowler. He will give us power to war against all Satan's cruel schemes. He will give us patience to withstand all his deadly influences.

God be praised for His promise to keep the feet of His saints from falling into the snares, traps, and pitfalls of Satan. At all times God is our Companion, sticking closer than a brother, and therefore able to make us more than conquerors.

21

An Acquaintance We Ne'er Forget

Now acquaint yourself with Him, and be at peace;
Thereby good will come to you (Job 22:21).

As the New Year comes round, we heartily sing the song that begins, "Should auld (old) acquaintance be forgot." How grateful we are that we have earthly alliances that are ever green in memory!

Samuel Johnson once wrote, "The shepherd in Virgil grew at long last acquainted with Love, and found him a native of the rocks." Once we become acquainted with the Love that will not let us go, we prove it to be of a rocklike character.

In his answer to what had gone before, Eliphaz the Temanite gave to Job a discourse on the character of the wicked. He affirmed that Job himself was a sinner who needed to be reconciled to God. For the Bible student, Job 22:21 provides a forceful message on the necessity of and on the blessings accruing from a decision to know and experience the saving power of Jesus. It is one of the most imposing texts to use when dealing with sinners. Of course, this was the way Eliphaz employed it. He assumed that Job was a sinner and that his trials and chastisements were an evidence that he needed to find God and to be at peace with Him. But such an approach was as untrue as it was unjust. It is distinctly stated that Job "feared God and shunned evil" (1:1). But when stripped of his material gains, he lamented that all his acquaintances, his close relatives, and his friends became completely estranged from him (see 19:9,11–21).

Although the premise of Eliphaz concerning the character of Job was false, what he did say about him was couched in some of the most eloquent, exquisite, and beautiful language to be found in literature. In such a captivating exhortation, Eliphaz sought to show what he meant by the necessity of Job's being reconciled to God (see 22:21–23) and to illustrate the happy and beneficial results of such a reconciliation, namely, peace and plenty (see 22:24–30).

Let us now examine the three aspects of the call of Eliphaz to Job to get right with God.

"Acquaint yourself with Him." The word *acquaint* and kindred terms are used in several different ways in Scripture. The Suffering Servant has an acquaintance with grief (see Is. 53:3). In his forecast of Judas, David wrote of his being the Lord's companion and acquaintance (see Ps. 55:12–14). Near His death, Jesus' friends and followers are referred to as "His acquaintances" (Luke 23:49). As He died upon the cross, these acquaintances stood at a distance and watched Him die. The word itself means "to know," "knowable," "to dwell," or "to associate with one." Thus, Albert Barnes in his *Commentary of Job* stated:

> Secure the friendship of God—become truly acquainted with Him. Be reconciled to Him. You are now estranged—you have no just views of Him—you murmur and complain—you are suffering under His displeasure as a *sinner*. But it is not too late to repent, and to return to Him and in so doing you will find peace.

Although the sense of the passage indicates a correct knowledge of one's true character and a necessary reconciliation with God, as we have already pointed out, this argument of Eliphaz against Job was most unwarranted.

"Be at peace." Job had no need of such advice, for he knew what it was to have his tent "in peace" (5:24). His delight was ever "in the Almighty" (22:26). Fundamentally, of course, there cannot be peace of heart and mind if a person's life is not fully reconciled to God. Such peace, perfect peace, can only come through the reception of the blood of the Cross. There is no peace so full of joy as that which results from complete harmony with the will of God and acquiescence in all the claims of God.

"Thereby good will come to you." This last phrase assures us of the benefits resulting from a right relationship with God, producing His divine favor in spiritual and temporal blessings. Examine this *good* flowing from oneness with God; it includes these blessings:

A full pardon and forgiveness from all past sin
A peace of conscience once remorseful because of
    secret and overt sins
An assurance that because of reconciliation with God,
    His benediction will be ours
A final triumph over death and the grave
An inclusion in the resurrection of the just
A crown incorruptible and undefiled in Heaven
An eternal worship and service for Him by whom we
    were reconciled to God.

Life for us now is "a heaven below, and a heaven above," and thus we are filled with a glorious hope.

22

Death—The Door into Life

For I know that You will bring me to death,
And to the house appointed for all living (Job 30:23).

The greatest mystery of life is the end of life. In the summary of his defense against the charge of wickedness leveled against him, Job indicated three verities about the mystery of death.

1. *The Divinity of Death.* "You will bring me to death." At Creation, God is revealed not only as the Source of all life, but also as the One producing death (see Gen. 3:3). As humans we ascribe death to many causes—sickness, disease, accident, and age. But the Bible ascribes it to God. Nothing else can bring us to death against His will. Our existence depends upon Him Who, moment by moment, gives physical and spiritual life from above. Nothing can prevent our dying when God's call comes to us to depart and be with Christ, which will be far better than life on earth. In God's purpose, there are no premature deaths.

2. *The Ordination of Death.* Death is no chance matter but is appointed. Scripture states this fact: "It is appointed for men to die once" (Heb. 9:27). Such an appointment is necessary and is seen in this planet—plants, reptiles, birds, insects, fish, and beasts, as well as human beings. For those saved by grace, there is the blessed promise of the Rapture. When Christ appears, living Christians will be caught up to meet Him in the

air and will escape the taste of death "O joy, O delight, should we go without dying." And we may!

3. *The Universality of Death*. Job comprehends that the appointment "for all living is death." Here on earth, people have houses of various structures, sizes, and values, according to their tastes and money. But in dying they have only one house—the grave! The grave, however, is not the final abode of the dead. For the child of God, the sky, not the grave, is the goal. But for all who die out of Christ, the grave is the door into everlasting condemnation. "Anyone not found written in the Book of Life was cast into the lake of fire" (Rev. 20:15).

23

A Fight We Cannot Win

Why do you contend with Him? (Job 33:13).

It is utter futility and folly for a creature to contend with the Creator, but such a conflict is frequently described in Scripture.

Isaiah pronounced a woe against all those who strive against their Maker, Who made the earth and created man on it (see Is. 45:9–13). What hope has a dwarf against a mighty giant?

As believers, we can be guilty of striving against the doctrines of God and against the dispensations of His providence. We can question, even scold. But such contention is rebellious, for God is perfect and thus He is not accountable to any. Daniel affirms this truth:

He does according to His will in the army of heaven
And among the inhabitants of the earth.
No one can restrain His hand
Or say to Him, "What have You done?" (Dan. 4:35).

Zechariah reminded us of our attitude when we confront and question some of the doings of our God Who can never make a mistake, "Be silent, all flesh, before the LORD" (Zech. 2:13). Where we cannot trace Him, we must trust Him Whose ways are always righteous and Whose wisdom is infinite. Although some of His methods appear to be mysterious ("Now we see in a mirror

147

dimly" [1 Cor. 13:12]) and His dispensations try the flesh, His designs are always precious and beneficial. Therefore, God commands our acquiescence on the basis of His perfection and promises.

Often a human father takes an action for a reason that his child cannot understand or that the father may deem proper to withhold from his child. Similarly, Jesus said to Simon Peter, at the washing of feet, "What I am doing you do not understand now, but you will know after this" (John 13:7).

That God "does not give an accounting of any of His words" (Job 33:13) implies that it is as useless as it is improper to fight against Him. He deals with a human being as He deems best and right. He has no reason to state the reasons of His doings, even in those things afflicting us. Thus when He does afflict individuals, permitting trials and sufferings to overtake us, and we cannot understand all our tears, we must submit to God's sovereign will. We must believe that though we cannot discern the reasons why He has permitted adverse circumstances to overtake us, we have a responsibility to submit to God's unerring purpose. We will not impose our knowledge of what we think is best.

Without question, God often presents Himself in clouds and thick darkness to test whether ours is sufficient confidence in Him. We must believe that He knows what is best and what is right, even though we cannot fathom the reason for what He permits or performs. Remember the father who sees reasons for his actions that his child cannot understand or that may be proper for him to withhold from his offspring.

Job perceived that man cannot contend with God. In response to God's power and majesty, Job, at the conclusion of this drama, proclaimed God's omnipotence. "You can do everything" (42:1). Job described his new understanding in terms of listening—not questioning—and in terms of new vision, "Now my eye sees You" (42:5).

Such knowledge gained from suffering has been expressed in these words:

> Not now, but in the coming years,
>   It may be in the better land.
> We'll read the meaning of our tears
>   And then someday, we'll understand.

24

God Does Not Pay According to our Terms

Should He repay it according to your terms,
Just because you disavow it?
You must choose, and not I;
Therefore speak what you know (Job 34:33).

In this magnificent speech, Elihu virtually said to Job, "Do you suppose that God will manage His government according to thy mind?" The general sense of such a question is that God will not be regulated or governed in His dealings by what may be the views of human beings. God ever acts according to His own views or standard of what is right and proper. A human being should not expect that He will consult the mind and feelings of humans rather than His own. He visits with good or evil, prosperity or adversity, according as He shall judge to be just and right.

Although the appeal of Elihu to Job was stated with magnificence, he included some sentiments divinely true and expressed with remarkable clarity, vigor, and sublimity. But Elihu misunderstood Job's character and reasoned with him in wrong and unjustifiable language. In his approach to Job, Elihu indicated that there is a tendency in human nature to adopt a position that is both irrational and immoral. His message is to them who are dissatisfied with the procedure of heaven and dare to sit in judgment upon the Most High.

Those among us who constantly murmur under the

dispensations of Providence and who think and say that things should be otherwise should remember these four ideas:

1. The circumscribed sphere of their observation is not universal. This earth of ours is a small spot, a mere atom in God's great universe. All who would decide things according to their own minds should comprehend God's government of heaven and earth.

2. Man should never forget the limitation of his human faculties as one who came from dust. In his own little sphere, how can he penetrate the full significances of all the issues and claims of his own small spot on earth?

3. Further, man should never forget the brevity of his mortal existence: "Here today, gone tomorrow." The universe began in eternity and has reached through millennia, but our sojourn here is for but a few years. Because of the uncertainty of the years we may have, we should live in the light of eternity.

4. How grateful we are that the work of redemption was not left according to our minds! There are those who try to form their scheme of spiritual restoration. But the fact remains that man cannot be saved from sin's penalty and power by his own works—only by the blood of Him Who died for our sins. The world by its own wisdom and works can never know God as He is fully revealed in His own Word.

The conclusion of this whole matter is that we cannot fashion a religion according to *our own* minds. We are utterly unsuited to construct a religion redemptive in its nature to man and acceptable to God Who created man. God never consults the views and feelings of man. He ever acts according to His *own* will, in the visitation of good or evil, prosperity or adversity, as He judges to be right. How assuring it is to rest by faith in the declaration of Isaiah:

> Since the beginning of the world
> Men have not heard nor perceived by the ear,
> Nor has the eye seen any God beside You,
> Who acts for the one who waits for Him (Is. 64:4; see
> 1 Cor. 2:9).

25

Request and Resolve

Teach me what I do not see;
If I have done iniquity, I will do no more (Job 34:32).

You find frequent and varied prayers in the Book of
Job. None of these prayers is more personal and practical than the one Elihu offered for divine instruction.
What Elihu the intercessor did not see was the iniquity
he resolved never to be guilty of again. Once he had
seen himself in the light of God's countenance, he
wanted to be free of sin. Whether unknown or willfully
violated, Elihu desired the hidden sin to become
known. Although he was not conscious of aggressively
violating God's law, the sin was there. Once the sin was
exposed as "a young lion lurking in secret places" (Ps.
17:12), he would sin in such a way no more.

Among the different words used of sin, the term *iniquity* is found some three hundred times in Scripture as a
whole, thirty times in the Book of Job. Iniquity implies a
wicked act of the mind, a delight in evil, and a willing
violation of God's law.

No prayer is more appropriate for us than this to offer
in regard to the sins we are liable to be guilty of. We
should be found entreating God to make us fully acquainted with transgressions of heart and life. Such a
discovery is the only way to profit from our guilt and
trials. When the unknown within us becomes known
and repented of, then such an action transforms all our

155

complaints and losses into a doxology (see Job 33:24; 35:10–11).

An impressive feature of the prayer before us is the recognition of God as a Teacher. Elihu asked the question, "Where is God . . . who teaches us. . . ?" (35:10–11). Here we have a sincere desire for a revelation of the machinations of the hidden old nature ever with us. No matter what good we may aspire to, we must have a God so loving and patient in His constant effort that He will forgive and instruct us in the way we should go. Alas! however, we are slow and sometimes unwilling to be taught of the Lord. Our constant cry should be "light," "more light," and "still more light." Every saint should strive to be a scholar in the divine school under the instruction of the greatest of all teachers, the Holy Spirit, Whom Jesus sent to "teach you all things" (John 14:26).

Every time we come to God's Word, our prayer should be: "Open my eyes, that I may see/Wondrous things from Your law" (Ps. 119:18). Give attention to the phrase "from Your law." The "things" are already in it and have always been there. But usually in family devotions or in our reading of Scripture, we read just the naked words as they appear. Somehow their inner, spiritual significance does not leap out of the page to grip our minds. The inherent truth fails to arrest us.

We need to find the depth of meaning in personal Bible study. We need to pray: Open my eyes, that I may see.

Elihu discovered that truth has a purifying effect. Jesus strongly emphasized the same idea in His message on the vine and branches: "You are already clean because of the word which I have spoken to you" (John 15:3). Then in His prayer of intercession for His disciples, He requested, "Sanctify them by Your truth. Your word is truth" (John 17:17). How blessed we are if, with the psalmist, we too can confess, "Your word I have hidden in my heart,/That I might not sin against You" (Ps. 119:11).

> I rest upon Thy word;
>   Thy promise is for me;
> My succour and salvation, Lord,
>   Shall surely come from Thee.

26

The Glory and Mystery of God

Where were you when I laid the foundations of the
  earth?
Tell Me, if you have understanding (Job 38:4).

People are attracted to a mystery. Busy statesmen re-
lax by reading a mystery book at bedtime. Tourists visit
Loch Ness, hoping to glimpse the mysterious monster.
Others visit Stonehenge and speculate about how the
enormous stones were placed in that circle in prehistoric
times; some even solve the mystery in a ridiculous way
by believing the stones were put there by visitors from
outer space. Indeed, there is much about life that is
mysterious.

The mystery of the Book of Job is that it points to a
greater mystery. The first puzzle is that it does not di-
rectly answer the question of suffering; Job received no
direct answers to his questions. The book points to the
greater mystery in the revelation of the nature of God
and His unfathomable universe.

Job, during his previous speeches, had voiced many
questions. In arrogance, he even went so far as to say to
God, "Let me speak, then You respond to me" (13:22).

Late in the book, God finally responded, but not in a
way Job expected. God said to Job, "I will question you,
and you shall answer Me" (38:3). God turned Job's re-
quest around, his own language against him.

Through almost four chapters of vivid imagery, from

the singing of angels at Creation to the ostrich leaving her eggs, the Creator pointed to puzzling glory. God made the point that a person cannot understand every part of life. The first of the divine speeches (38:1–40:2) emphasized the wisdom of God in Creation. The second speech (40:6–42:34) dealt with the Creator's power over Creation.

Several times Job had said to his friends he wanted to present his case in the heavenly court. But once God appeared on the scene, He overwhelmed Job with His wisdom and power. The first divine question was devastating: Who is this ignorant questioner? The second was similar: Where were you when I created the earth and the sea? In a series of continuing questions, God showed that only He could operate the universe, doing such things as storing up snow to use later in battle. Then God pointed to animals—lions, mountain goats, the wild ass, the wild ox, the strange ostrich, the mighty war-horse, the hawk, and the eagle.

The Divine Speaker paused. Then followed a brief confession from humbled Job. God continued to challenge the man. He spoke of behemoth and leviathan. These could be the hippopotamus and the crocodile. Yet their descriptions allude to great size and beastly power—similar to those of the Loch Ness monster, completely mysterious except to God and completely untameable except by God.

Notice that God presented his list of mysteries with a question. Job was asked if he were present at Creation,

When the morning stars sang together,
And all the sons of God shouted for joy? (Job 38:7).

What a delightful reference to stars you find in the Creation record, "He made the stars *also*" (Gen. 1:16, italics added). After the fashioning of the two great lights, the sun and the moon, God did not forget the gimlet holes in the heavens to let the glory through. With a word, He brought the myriads of brilliant stars into being. The marvel is that the Lord brought forth the host of the stars by number, and "calls them all by name" (Is. 40:26). Our finite minds cannot grasp the reality of such divine knowledge. God has a particular name for each star as it shines and sings, "The Hand that made us is Divine!"

One is impressed with the description that the morning stars sing "together." In such a heavenly choir there is never a note out of place, never a discord, never a lack of harmony. Unison in song is perfect. As with one voice, the jubilant choir accomplishes its chief end of glorifying God.

As the son of the morning, morning stars are before others. The day is born of them. With the rising of the sun, the stars become invisible to the naked eye. The expression "the morning stars" is used because of the beauty of the principal star which, at certain seasons of the year, leads on to morning.

"The sons of God shouted for joy" (38:7). This designation refers to angels, not to men. Soul-winning will later bring similar angelic jubilation, as Jesus affirmed when He declared, "There will be more joy in heaven over one sinner who repents than over ninety-nine just persons who need no repentance" (Luke 15:7).

The angels are called *stars*, seeing they are joined with them in extolling God for His power in Creation, Providence, and Redemption. No wonder they "shouted for joy," a joy unspeakable and full of glory! The angelic choir praised God for His glorious work in the creation of a new world—an event most fitting to honor God. The Creation manifested a new demonstration of His glorious power, an enlargement of His empire, and also an exhibition of benevolence that claimed angelic gratitude.

When the world was made by God, it was beautiful, pure, lovely, and holy. Man was made like unto his God, and all Creation was full of love. It was to be a world that was worth creating and worth redeeming.

The Creator set boundaries for His world:

When I said,
"This far you may come, but no farther,
And here your proud waves must stop!" (Job 38:11).

Whenever I have the opportunity of standing on a seashore, I am always fascinated by the wonderful, constant movements of the mighty ocean. It proudly rolls in on the beach as if it would sweep everything away. Then the waters are checked by a divinely ordered barrier, for a voice seems to say to them, "You may roll in with all your pride and grandeur to this point, but no farther." God has fixed limits, and so the proud waters are stayed and made to recede. In a moment they are prostrate at the feet of their Creator.

How grateful to God we are that He never rolls a burden upon us too heavy to bear. He never forces us beyond the limits set for us! He knows the very moment the proud waves must stop—and He stops them! How rich is the promise, "God is faithful, who will not allow you to be tempted beyond what you are able, but with the temptation will also make the way of escape, that you may be able to bear it" (1 Cor. 10:13). In all permitted satanic testing, there is the divine proviso, "This far you may come, but no farther." He Who governs the heavenly bodies that rule the earth's tides also functions as the Director of man's life on earth.

May trust and confidence in the over-ruling Providence of God in all things be ours! He is able to make all things, even the most untoward experience, work together for our good.

> All is most right
> That seems most wrong
> If it be His sweet will.

All of this description simply showed Job the greatness of his God. Job responded to the confrontation with utter submission. He was overwhelmed by his own smallness in contrast to the omnipotence of the Almighty. The mystery and glory of God brought him to a personal, face-to-face encounter. Beyond hearsay, he had experienced the Almighty and could be a witness for Him.

Job did not have his specific questions answered. God refused to do so. His loving Son also refused on occasions to answer (see John 19:9). But when Job discovered the greatness of God and His created universe, he was silenced. Job saw his own finitude. He knew the bounds of his own ignorance. But the mystery and glory he experienced pushed him out into deeper waters of reverence and toward further horizons of hope.

27

Wisdom from the Animal Realm

Will the unicorn be willing to serve thee, or abide by thy crib? (Job 39:9 KJV).

The wings of the ostrich wave proudly,
But are her wings . . . like the kindly stork's? (Job 39:13).

Previously God pointed out the lion, the raven, the goats, the hind, and the wild ass, whose instincts prove His wisdom. He now turns to the unicorn and the ostrich, two of the strangest of His creations.

The unicorn is an unusual animal, displaying God's power in its great strength and independence. The unicorn, because of its fierceness, is mentioned also in Deuteronomy, Psalms, and Isaiah.

Doubt prevails among scholars as to the exact identity of this animal. Jerome translated it as *rhinoceros*, a view generally held. Most modern translators treat it as the wild *ox*. What is clearly evident from Scripture is the fact that nowhere is it intimated that the animal had only *one* horn.

The main characteristics of the unicorn are its great strength and untameableness. It cannot be used, as with the tame ox, for agricultural purposes. Its willing service cannot be expected for harrowing the land and carrying home "your grain . . . to your threshing floor" (39:12). Because of its enormous size and strength, it cannot be domesticated so that after a hard day's toil it is content to abide or dwell in its barn at night.

The question, Can you bind the unicorn with his head "in the furrow?" (39:10), indicates the common traces or cords employed in the binding of oxen to the plow. As to the harrowing of "the valleys," the thought is of such ground capable of being plowed or harrowed. Hills and mountains cannot be cultivated in this way. The phrase, "Will you trust him because his strength is great?" (39:11), implies that the beast is untamed, unsubdued, and ungovernable. Its great strength cannot be trusted for field work. With the ox, camel, horse, and even the elephant, it was different; the reason man used them was for doing what he himself was not able to do. A rhinoceros or a wild ox cannot be employed for the same purpose of production of a field. If sheaves of the harvest were laid on him, it would be doubtful they would ever reach the threshing floor.

Now let us proceed in our meditation to the ostrich and her feathery wings. Among the many pleasurable and profitable themes of the Bible to meditate upon is that of *wings*, not only of birds, but of God and His messengers. A symbol of speed and protection, wings are His swift envoys.

Previously, Job touched upon the wild and untameable animals of the desert; but in verse 13 before us, he alluded to the feathered tribes, distinguished by their strength or fleetness of wing as an evidence of the power, wisdom, and Providence of God. As Barnes expressed it,

> The idea is, that these animals, far away from the abodes of men, where it could not be pretended that man had anything to do with their training, had habits and instincts peculiar to themselves, which showed great variety in the divine plans and at the same time consummate wisdom.

Often, when trials, disappointments, failures, and problems overtake us, we find ourselves sighing with the psalmist, "Oh, that I had wings like a dove!/For then I would fly away and be at rest" (Ps. 55:6).

28

A Gate into Glory

Have the gates of death been revealed to you?
Or have you seen the doors of the shadow of death? (Job
38:17).

As I set out to meditate on the above verses, I realize
that at the advanced age of ninety-seven, I will soon see
those gates. If the Rapture does not occur within the
near future, the gates of death will open for me to enter
into the Father's home, there to see the King in all His
beauty—and what a gate into everlasting joy and peace
that will prove to be!

The almost two hundred Scripture references to *gates*
provide an aspect of truth not generally dealt with. As a
fitting introduction to such a profitable theme, Cruden
in his *Concordance* has the following preface to his list of
verses where gates are mentioned:

> The gates were the important part of an ancient city.
> They gave the only means of passing through the wall
> and were usually closed at night and were strengthened
> by bars of brass or iron. The gate was the place of public
> concourse, partly because it was an open space, not usu-
> ally found elsewhere in a city. Much of the legal business
> of the city was done there, Ruth 4:11. The word *gate* is
> sometimes used to mean power or dominion. God prom-
> ises Abraham that his posterity should possess the gates
> of their enemies, their towns, their fortresses, Gen.
> 22:17. They should conquer them, they should have do-
> minion over them.

As for "the gates of death," the brink or the mouth of the grave is implied. "The shadow of death" is a phrase frequently used to denote the deepest darkness, the abode of departed spirits, described by Job as the place where "light is like darkness" (10:21–22). The idea conveyed is that death was a dark and gloomy object that obstructed all light. Job presented a great variety of forms and phrases to depict the land of darkness as being total and absolute night—a place where not a ray of light ever shines—the Hades of the ancients. John Milton used similar language: "A vast immeasurable abyss . . . dark, wasteful void."

The gates of death, now hoary with age, were first opened by the sinning of our first parents, Adam and Eve. Their sin became the parent of death and raised great and gloomy gates, investing "dying with a darkness as a hundred midnights."

All is not dark, though. Consider the hope in these words: "O Death, I will be your plagues!/O Grave, I will be your destruction!" (Hos. 13:14). And in these: "He will swallow up death forever" (Is. 25:8). The Apostle Paul must have had such prophecies in mind when he wrote: "O Death, where is your sting?/O Hades, where is your victory?" (1 Cor. 15:55).

With the advent of Christianity, believers learned of a brighter world beyond the grave—a world that is all light, fashioned by Him who became "the Light of the world," a clear Light now shining around the grave and beyond it where, because there is no night, all is light and one bright eternal day.

John Howe reminded us that, "There is a key and a key—a key to let us out of earth, and a key to let us into the unseen." Is it not wonderful to have Him who destroyed the Devil and the power of death as the Arbiter of our destiny?

If only Job had been favored with the possession of the New Testament with its full and final revelation of heaven, he would have had a brighter hope and no fear of death. In this way, we are more fortunate than Job.

29

From Nature to Nature's God

Have you entered the treasury of snow,
Or have you seen the treasury of hail . . . ?
Who has divided a channel for the overflowing water,
Or a path for the thunderbolt,
To cause it to rain on a land where there is no one,
A wilderness in which there is no man . . . ?
Has the rain a father?
Or who has begotten the drops of dew? . . .
And the frost of heaven, who gives it birth? (Job 38:22, 25–29).

When the patriarch listened to his Creator, he was overwhelmed by the references to the realms of Nature and human life. He was impressed by these symbols of divine truths. This effect seems to be the one that God sought.

As we study some of these figures from Nature, let us try to learn from them. Shakespeare described people who found

. . tongues in trees, books in the running brooks,
Sermons in stones, and good in everything.
—*As You Like It*, II, 1

The Lord assured Job that treasures can be found even in such unwelcome aspects of Nature as snow and hail. During the winter when there has been a heavy fall of snow and we have to shovel hard to clear a pathway from our door, we do not think of the unwelcome snow as a treasure. Yet here is God saying that snow is laid up as a treasure and kept in reserve until He deigns to use it. He did not set out to give Job a scientific explanation of the phenomena of Nature in the formation of beautiful snowflakes, or how they are formed to fulfill His purpose. They simply execute His mission. Science, however, informs us that "snow is congealed vapor, formed in the air by the vapor being frozen there before it appears in crystal form as white snow." The more intricate the creation the more honor goes to the Creator.

The treasures of the snow, then, lie in its extreme beauty and variety, and in the benefits it bestows upon the earth. The treasures of hail are not quite as obvious.

What are these further treasures that can be seen? Some time ago a severe hailstorm overtook our city, and as the large hailstones pounded the roof of my mobile home, I failed to see where their treasure lay.

The stones themselves consist of masses of ice, or frozen vapor, falling from the clouds in beautiful crystallized forms.

A treasury of hail, the formation of which was probably unknown to Job in his day, is seen as an evidence of God's superior power and wisdom. The Creator can use this treasury when and how He deems necessary. Thus, hail is called upon to praise God, because it fulfills His Word and purpose in troubled times.

In addition to snow and hail, the Lord reminded Job of several aspects of the natural world, namely, floods, thunder, rain, dew, and frost.

Waters that flow down from the heavens do not pour down in floods, but flow in certain canals formed for them, as if they had been cut out through the clouds for that purpose. "He binds up the waters in His thick clouds" (26:8). God appears to collect the waters in the clouds, as in bottles or vessels.

The companions of lightning and thunder are often

given in Scripture as being the voice of God in power. Lightning is described as "the fire of God" falling from heaven and burning up the sheep of Job (1:16). Who but the Almighty God could trace out a path for the thunderflash to travel along? "Then sings my soul, my Savior God to Thee; How great Thou art!"

That God is the Father or Creator of rain is proven by His own statement, "I will cause it to rain on the earth" (Gen. 7:4). The land had regular rain except when God withheld it as a form of chastisement. Scripture reveals that rain is used both in a good and in a bad sense. The particular aspect of the ministry of rain is that God causes it to fall on uninhabited and barren wilderness areas of the earth, which fact heightens the conception of the power of God.

There is a great fascination in the whole description of God as the Source of the falling rain far away from human habitation. God makes it rain in the lonely wastes, resulting in the springing up of tender herbs and blooming flowers. The law of Nature was doubtless unknown to Job, a law only known to the all-wise Author of Nature. Rain, falling on the sandy desert or on the barren rock, may appear wasted to man. But to God it is of value, designed to accomplish some necessary purpose.

Dew is a gift of God, a refreshment provided by Him and withheld for punishment or discipline (38:26–28). During the summer, dew is copious in Palestine and greatly aids in the cultivation of the land. Dew is, therefore, symbolic of the spiritual refreshment God provides for us during the night of our Lord's absence from the earth.

As the dew sweetly refreshes and cheers the earth when scorched and dried up by the sun's intemperate heat, so the Lord, through His own, makes them as fruitful as the dew does the earth.

The hoary frost gives birth to the ice and is a further proof of the wisdom of God. Referred to as resulting from "the breath of God" (37:10), frost is not caused by violent north winds or by whirlwinds from the south. It is breathed in a gentle manner as it covers the earth. The figure of *breath* is as poetical as it is beautiful. It appears in the still night when there is no storm or tempest, and it covers the earth as silently as if it were breathing. Actually, frost is congealed or frozen dew. The slight motion of the air, even when the frost appears, is described as the breathing of God. How such a fact exalts our conceptions of the wisdom and greatness of God!

Let us move, as Job did, from contemplating Nature to worshiping Nature's God.

30

The Rewards of Prayer

The LORD turned the captivity of Job, when he prayed
for his friends: also the LORD gave Job twice as much as
he had before (Job 42:10 KJV).

One cannot linger long with Job without being spiritually enriched by his reverential trust in God, his
hatred of evil, and his assurance that the Lord, as the
Redeemer, would ultimately stand upon the earth as its
Governor.

The Hebrew word for *captivity* used in verse 10 is not
to be understood in the sense of bondage. It means
what was captured from Job. The New King James Version translates it, "The LORD restored Job's losses."

By divine permission, Satan was allowed to afflict
Job's bones and flesh. For seven days and seven nights,
he suffered excruciating pain and discomfort from his
boil-covered body; he was robbed of physical action and
mental peace. But Job never lost his faith in God. All he
had lost by his week's suffering was fully restored. He
triumphantly emerged from his series of protracted trials in a state of prosperity.

The immediate action of Job's restoration was to pray
for his friends. Please note that such intercession was
not the basis of such a restoration. The verse should
read, "After this he prayed for his friends." Such prayer
resulted in the bestowal of the Lord's favor. In His commission to Eliphaz the Temanite to approach Job, God's

condemning him contrasted his unworthiness to Job's uprightness and affirmed, "My servant Job shall pray for you. For I will accept him" (42:8).

Functioning as an officiating priest, Job is "a beautiful instance of the nature and propriety of intercession for others. Job was a holy man; his prayers would be acceptable to God, and his friends were permitted to avail themselves of his powerful intercession in their behalf." Barnes, in his *Commentary*, further stated:

It is also an instance showing the nature of the patriarchal worship. It did not consist merely in offering sacrifices. Prayer was to be connected with sacrifices, nor is there any evidence that bloody offerings were regarded as available in securing acceptance with God, except in connection with fervent prayer. It is also an instance showing the nature of patriarchal piety.

Who were the three "friends" Job was ready to pray for? They were the three who "comforted" him when the adversity of boils covered his body, namely, Eliphaz the Temanite, Bildad the Shuhite, and Zophar the Naamathite. Solomon's injunction reads, "A man who has friends must himself be friendly" (Prov. 18:24). Job was the personification of true friendship—an attribute his so-called friends lacked, as their record proved.

Think of the ways they grieved their loyal friend by their severe reproaches. Recall how confidently they persisted that Job was not blameless and upright, as he was declared to be, but eminently a bad man. But manifesting forgiveness, he was ready to welcome these professed friends to association with him in an act of worship. Job, in his far-off day, was an example of a Christ-like virtue, for he knew how to heap coals of fire on the heads of his unfriendly friends.

We are to pray one for another. Such mutual intercession binds us closer to Him "Who ever liveth to make intercession." And as Alexander Smellie reminded us, "When Job's captivity was turned, he passed out of his winter into spring, as he besought the grace of God for his friends."

Job's heartfelt prayers had a further result, for the verse concludes with a double benediction, "The LORD gave Job twice as much as he had before" (42:10). How benevolent is the God we adore. He is ever ready to give more than we could possibly ask for or receive! He is never miserly in His giving. The prediction to Job through Bildad must have been comforting, "Though your beginning was small,/Yet your latter end would increase abundantly" (8:7). Dwell on that word *abundantly*. It describes God's way. Jesus assured His disciples that He came, not only that they might have life, but "have it *more abundantly*" (John 10:10, italics added).

The reader's impression from these marvelous rewards should not be to exclaim, "How great Job was" but "How great Job's God was and is." I close this little volume with the hope that readers will continue to open their hearts to the greatness of God our Creator, to accept the atonement of Christ our Redeemer, and to follow the day-by-day leadership of the Holy Spirit our Comforter.

www.ingramcontent.com/pod-product-compliance
Ingram Content Group UK Ltd.
Pitfield, Milton Keynes, MK11 3LW, UK
UKHW02080912032 5
456141UK00001B/30